A Diary of Dreams, Visions & Revelations

A. M. Wright
A Diary of Dreams, Visions & Revelations

Published by Spines
ISBN 979-8-89569-332-2

A Diary of Dreams, Visions & Revelations

A. M. Wright

CONTENTS

Foreword 7

Introduction 9

1. Hell's Flame Fires 17
2. Devil On Assignment 61
3. The Vision 79
4. The Encounter 95
5. Stay in the Car 101
6. It Began Below Ground 115
7. The Manhole 121
8. Thus, My Heart was Grieved 125
9. Natural Progression - The Conveyor Belt of Life 143
10. Do Not Be Deceived 151
11. Ancient Demonic Spirits 171
12. The Tragedy of Blind Allegiance 179
13. Shorts 185
14. The Winding Down Of The Matter 207

Notes 211

Foreword

It is with great honor and distinct pleasure that I write the foreword for my mother's new book, which serves as a profound exploration of God's purpose for our lives and the eternal questions of existence. Her unwavering faith and dedication to prayer have been a guiding light not only in my life but in the lives of countless others. Throughout her journey, she has been a source of encouragement and strength, an anchor in the storm, and, without hesitation, continues to pray fervently for those in need.

In this book, my mother delves into the mysteries of divine purpose and invites readers to reflect on their own spiritual journeys. Through scripture and personal reflections, she reveals how our lives unfold within God's divine plan, reminding us that we are never alone.

Her profound reflections on divine encounters and the beauty of sharing Christ's light with others are potent reminders of the importance of accepting the invitation to salvation. They challenge us to embrace genuine repentance and transformation. Her insights into the power of God's

Word and the profound truths in John 3:16–19 inspire us to live with purpose and passion, guiding us to a deeper understanding of our faith and mission.

Truly, this book is a testament to her unwavering faith and a heartfelt invitation for all readers to deepen their relationship with God and embrace the hope and promise of eternity. I sincerely hope this work will encourage you as it has encouraged me, illuminating your path to divine understanding and spiritual fulfillment. May it serve as a beacon of light, guiding you toward a deeper connection with God and a more profound sense of purpose.

Nat Simone, CEO and vocal artist.
Nat Simone Music
(561) 840-5603
www.natsimonemusic.com
natsimonemusic@pm.me

Introduction

Within the intricacy of our existence, each of us carries a storyline—a purpose uniquely ours. To know and understand God's purpose for our lives is to unravel the profound question of our existence. As a Believer, I hold the conviction that nothing in our lives unfolds by mere coincidence; rather, it aligns with God's divine plan. Once we place our lives in the Master's hands, the concept of coincidence dissipates, and our true purpose unfolds with clarity and grace.

Indeed, our life journeys are as unique as our fingerprints. Each pain we endure becomes a steppingstone to strength and resilience. In the crucible of suffering, we are meticulously shaped by the Potter's hands, transforming us into vessels of honor and purpose.

While I understand that not everyone will grasp or embrace the intricacies of this non-fiction account, I am pleased to boldly express the profound truths that my dear Heavenly Father, through the leadership of the Holy Spirit, has lovingly instilled within me. My testimony is woven with experiences that have deepened my faith in the one true God. These experiences are etched within the depths of my spirit, serving as a testament to His unwavering love, forgiveness, patience and mercy, as exemplified in the following testimony:

On a rare day off from work several years ago, I felt an inexplicable nudge—an urge to visit a company where I had once worked; it was the voice of the Holy Spirit. Friends from my past still worked there, and my memories of them were warm. The nudging continued, but hesitancy embraced me.

As I traveled on the parkway, I knew I should exit the ramp close by the company, but I hesitated. As I approached the ramp, my car began experiencing mechanical issues—it sputtered, backfired, and then smoke started billowing from beneath the hood. I had no choice but to exit at the ramp.

I sat in the parking lot of the office building, which stood unchanged. Its façade, weathered but a monument to countless memories, remained. Inside, the air held echoes—conversations and laughter all suspended in time. But the memory of those sacred Tuesdays tugged at my heart. A distinct group of colleagues—diverse in roles—gathered in a conference room for prayer and Bible study.

The president of the corporation granted us permission to keep these meetings. The department heads frowned, yet we persisted. At noon, the room was transformed and became a sanctuary. We prayed for colleagues, families, the leadership of the company, and our nation.

And so, the old office building stood—where our prayers were offered to the Lord. Those hallowed Tuesdays left an indelible impression on all of us.

I sensed a divine appointment; I was there on a special

assignment to see Edna. Edna was a no-nonsense older woman of Jamaican heritage. She was a respected figure in the office who always had my back. Although I waited for the opportune moment to share my faith with her—and not just religion—she would deflect my attempts and circumvent the conversation.

Stepping into the familiar office building, I deliberately veered away from Edna's department; instead, I followed the path toward other departments where I had friends—even though I was fully aware that Edna was at work that day.

After a while, I left the echoing memories of the old office building behind. The car started immediately; the smoke had now cleared, and the water I poured into it earlier had cooled it down.

One week after my last visit to the company, the news arrived: Edna had suffered a massive heart attack while at home and passed away.

Regret weighed heavily upon me; I thought about the missed opportunities that I failed to take advantage of—those pivotal moments when I chose not to follow the leading of the Lord but to be silent instead.

The days that followed were heavy with sorrow and grief. I mourned the sudden loss of a dear friend who had passed away without warning. Despite the promptings of the Holy Ghost urging me to visit Edna, I hesitated and did not heed the call. On that fateful day, an epiphany washed over me that revealed something profound about myself.

As I grappled with an unsettling truth, I realized that my unease about seeing Edna stemmed from a deeper knowing, a deeper fear: I somehow knew that we were destined to meet each other for the very last time. The questions that troubled me were profound: "Did I have a word for her? Would she have accepted the Lord that day?" These troubling questions carved themselves deeply into my heart.

In the quiet solitude of my room, I knelt in earnest prayer, seeking both consolation and forgiveness. Tears blurred my vision as I poured out my heart to the Lord, confessing my feelings of inadequacy, regret, failures, and disobedience. Amidst my supplications, I fervently prayed that the Lord had sent someone to minister to Edna before she passed and that she had accepted the Lord Jesus Christ into her heart.

The warmth of God's presence and grace touched the chambers of my heart that day. I experienced profound cleansing and renewal. I also understood that my role is not to impose salvation upon anyone but to serve as a vessel—a witness to God's love and grace for all who are willing to listen.

Each of us carries a unique story of God's supernatural protection and provision within our hearts. These stories are compelling and vital, reminding us that we are not alone in our journey.

Today, I pray that the message within these pages stirs your heart and reignites the flame of faith within you. May it serve as a reminder of God's unwavering faithfulness and abundant provision. Our God remains steadfast, never abandoning us, even in the darkest hours.

Dedication

To my beloved family,
Your unwavering support and encouragement have been invaluable—thank you so much. Above all, I am profoundly indebted to the Precious Holy Spirit, whose presence has been a constant source of strength and comfort. In the quiet moments of doubt—and there have been many—and the peaks of inspiration, the Comforter has been my steadfast companion.
I offer my sincere thanks and gratitude for the divine experiences, gifts, and talents that have flowed through me. I could not have accomplished this undertaking without You! I extend this expression of appreciation for the grace that has guided each word and every sentence penned within these covers.
In the Blessed Name of Jesus.

*[15] That whosoever believeth in him should not perish, but
have eternal life.
[16] For God so loved the world, that he gave his only
begotten Son, that whosoever believeth in him should not
perish, but have everlasting life.
[17] For God sent not his Son into the world to condemn the
world; but that the world through him might be saved.
[18] He that believeth on him is not condemned: but he that
believeth not is condemned already, because he hath not
believed in the name of the only begotten Son of God.
[19] And this is the condemnation, that light is come into
the world, and men loved darkness rather than light
because their deeds were evil.
[20] For everyone that doeth evil hateth the light, neither
cometh to the light, lest his deeds should be reproved.*

— JOHN 3:15-20

Chapter 1

Hell's Flame Fires

Despite the weight of years upon his shoulders, David stood tall—a man of imposing stature. His very presence commanded respect, a political giant whose influence reached far and wide. Yet, beyond the public eye, he was a devoted husband, father, and grandfather. As a political advisor, he navigated the intricate currents of power while his heart remained anchored in faith as a Methodist minister. But, in the quiet and secret chambers of brotherhood, he bore the emblem of a Freemason. So, he was a figure both esteemed and cherished.

Upon our introduction, I was oblivious to the depths of his knowledge, the extensive network of his connections, and the influence and command he held over political dignitaries across the spectrum.

He evolved into more than just a mentor; he became a confidant and a cherished friend whose esteem I held in the highest regard. Whenever new revelations surfaced concerning the deceitful actions of the individual under the vigilant watch of our Board of Commissioners, David was my go-to source of wisdom and guidance. As a collective body, the Board of Commissioners felt a profound obligation to meticulously scrutinize every piece of evidence that came to light. Our ultimate objective was to ensure accountability, which led us to seek the termination of the party found at fault, in this case, the Executive Director.

At that point in time, I was unaware of another unfolding drama. As more information began to surface—thanks to the vigilant and conscientious efforts of our staff members who initially placed their trust in David before turning to me—it became apparent that the staff had reservations about the documents they were providing to David. They harbored a gnawing fear that he might choose to conveniently disregard these documents rather than bring them promptly to my attention. In a shocking turn of events, it was revealed that David was inextricably embroiled in the very web of corruption and deception that we were striving to unravel and rectify, even while serving as co-chair.

The documents that were brought to light were clandestinely distributed and circulated among his political allies. They realized that I had been made aware of their corruption. Unbeknownst to me, I had been singled out for retaliation and payback—an inevitable consequence of my audacious act of thwarting and impeding their lucrative and profitable schemes by exposing the deep-rooted corruption.

So, who was David in reality? He was a foe masquerading under a cloak of deception, skillfully feigning allegiance while meticulously documenting my every move for the upper echelons of authority.

Turning Point

The critical juncture was reached when we arranged a confidential meeting with the Executive Director, who was answerable to the Board of Commissioners, the person central to the misconduct. We intended to confront him with irrefutable proof of his calculated misallocation and misappropriation of the organization's funds.

Upon arrival at the office, David and the Executive Director exchanged heated words. David vehemently demanded that the Executive Director immediately disband the charitable organization from which he had been diverting funds. At the time, I did not fully understand that David, the Executive Director, and other high-ranking officials, including lawyers, judges, and a board member, were also entangled in the same corruption.

Seated at the expansive conference room table, I observed their fervent disagreement. The atmosphere was laden with almost palpable tension as both argued their points, which persisted until the two men took their seats.

The stern and unyielding Executive Director sat at the table's helm, a figure of authority, held his ground. His stern demeanor reflected his steadfast commitment to his stance.

Opposite me, my associate and co-chair, David, a person of equal determination, maintained his stance. His resolve was evident in his eyes. Once a battlefield of words and wills, the room stood silent for a moment, bearing the remnants of a dispute that had tested the fortitude of all present.

As David once again engaged the Executive Director, I sensed a subtle shift in the room's atmosphere. The ambiance transformed, and in that moment of revelation, I became acutely aware of an extraordinary phenomenon—an open vision unraveling before my eyes.

David's words gradually receded into the background as my mind raced to comprehend the magnitude of the experience unfolding before me.

Open Vision

An Open Vision occurs when an individual is fully awake rather than asleep. During this Open Vision, an extraordinary event unfolded before my eyes. Towering flames, reaching a height of four feet, erupted in a powerful display above David's head. Intense and mesmerizing radiant flames danced in a captivating blend of blue, white, yellow, and orange. Remarkably, they did not emanate from his head but hovered above it as if suspended in midair, defying the laws of nature.

Oblivious to the extraordinary vision that seized my complete attention, David continued to articulate his thoughts. Unaware of the fiery halo above his head, he remained engrossed in his discourse while I was held captive by the humbling spectacle unfolding before me.

The atmosphere was electrified, a potent charge permeating the air, yet this profound shift seemed to elude everyone in the room but me. In that moment of deep revelation, I felt a divine presence—the Holy Spirit of God spoke to me. The voice, resonating with an authority that commanded respect and wisdom that offered guidance, made a powerful declaration: *"HELL'S FLAME FIRES!"*

This declaration, stark and resounding, etched a permanent mark deep within the depths of my being. I knew it was the Spirit of God who helped me to remain calm. My head bowed instinctively, and a torrent of emotions cascaded from within, followed by a silent plea to my Heavenly Father. Tears welled up in my eyes as I cried out to God in silence: "Not him, Lord, please not him. I could come to terms with the Executive Director's fate, but not him, Lord, please not him."

I was initially unable to comprehend the situation. Prior to discovering David's involvement in corruption, I believed he epitomized goodness, kindness, and integrity. The shock and disbelief I experienced were overwhelming. This reminded me of the scripture in 1 Samuel 16:1-13, where the Lord teaches Samuel, the prophet, that appearances can be deceiving and that the heart truly matters.

Samuel, the esteemed Prophet of God, was in deep mourning for Saul, the first King of Israel, whom he had anointed to serve in that esteemed position. However, Saul had strayed from God's path and disobeyed His divine instructions. Consequently, the Lord addressed Samuel, saying, [1]*HOW LONG WILL YOU MOURN FOR SAUL, SEEING THAT I HAVE REJECTED HIM FROM REIGNING OVER ISRAEL?* The Lord then commanded Samuel to fill his horn with oil and go visit Jesse of Bethlehem, for among Jesse's sons, He had chosen a new king. (1 Samuel 16:1).

Upon arriving at Jesse's house, Jesse proudly presented his sons before Samuel. As the first son, Eliab, passed by, Samuel thought to himself: [6] *Surely the Lord's anointed is before him.* (1 Samuel 16:6).

Samuel was utterly convinced that Eliab would be God's anointed one. As Eliab approached, Samuel felt a surge of anticipation and certainty. He saw in Eliab the qualities of a king—strength, stature, and presence—that aligned perfectly with what he believed God would choose. The air was thick with expectation, and Samuel's heart pounded as he prepared to anoint Eliab. Suddenly, in a moment of divine intervention, the Lord spoke to Samuel, shattering his assumptions and adding a profound tension to the scene.

> [7] *LOOK NOT ON HIS COUNTENANCE, OR ON THE HEIGHT OF HIS STATURE; BECAUSE I HAVE REFUSED HIM: FOR THE LORD SEETH NOT AS MAN SEETH; FOR MAN LOOKETH ON THE OUTWARD APPEARANCE, BUT THE LORD LOOKETH ON THE HEART.*
>
> — 1 SAMUEL 16:7

When seven of Jesse's sons had been presented before Samuel, Samuel said unto Jesse, [11] *The Lord hath not chosen these. Are here all thy children?* (1 Samuel 16:11)

Jesse replied, [11] *There remaineth yet the youngest, and behold, he keepeth the sheep.* (1 Samuel 16:11)

And Samuel said unto Jesse, [11] *Send and fetch him: for we will not sit down until he comes hither.* (1 Samuel 16:11).

When David arrived and was presented before Samuel, he had a ruddy complexion and strikingly handsome features. His countenance reflected his inner strength and determination as a proctor of the flock. Shepherds were responsible for safeguarding their herd, which included slaying predatory animals and leading the sheep to still waters. Naturally, shepherds often had an unkept appearance due to their infrequent washing. Nevertheless, there was intense anticipation in the air as everyone watched this young shepherd stand before the prophet. It was then that the Lord spoke to Samuel, saying: [12] *Arise, anoint him: for this is he.* (1 Samuel 16:12).

King David would go on to become Israel's second king

and be in the lineage of Joseph, the stepfather of Jesus, who was married to Mary, the mother of Jesus.

The Lord God knows the heart of man and their true intentions:

> *[9] The heart is deceitful above all things, and desperately wicked: who can know it? [10] I, the Lord, search the heart, I try the reins, even to give every man according to his ways, and according to the fruit of his doings.*
>
> — JEREMIAH 17:9-10

While I lack the authority to condemn anyone to the inferno of hell, the stark reality of its existence has become increasingly tangible. The gravity of this truth weighs heavily upon me, more so now than ever before.

Suddenly, with speed as startling as their arrival, the flames abruptly vanished into thin air, leaving behind nothing but their unforgettable memory, etched into my mind with haunting clarity.

David concluded his argument, unaware of the inferno that appeared above his head; the executive director was also oblivious to the event that unfolded. But I knew I had glimpsed a message from the Holy Spirit that lingered: "Hell's flame fires."

David and I exited the building together. As he pulled up to my home, we remained seated in his vehicle in silence, lost in a sea of unspoken thoughts. The weight of the vision still clung to my mind. Though I yearned to share it with him, the words refused to come. Instead, I felt an urgent need to warn him, to convey the frailty and fleeting nature of our earthly existence. David, in his early eighties, needed to hear this truth, even if I could not reveal the vision of hell's flame fires at that very moment.

David, a man steeped in wisdom and rich with the passage of years, sat next to me—a vessel of life's experiences. Yet, in this moment, I felt an overwhelming urge to voice the burden that was pressing heavily upon my heart.

"David," I began, my voice trembling with urgency and emotion, "there's a matter of great importance I feel compelled to discuss." His gaze, filled with understanding and concern, shifted to meet mine. "Go on," he prompted, his tone gentle yet encouraging.

"David, life is so brief; it's but a fleeting moment, and then, just like that, it dissipates as swiftly as the blink of an eye. We must prepare ourselves for the inevitable encounter with our Creator, the Almighty God. This is a matter of eternal significance, and we cannot afford to ignore it." My voice wavered as I spoke, the weight of the words pressing heavily on my heart. "We must be ready, David. We must make sure our hearts are right with Him."

Then, driven by the divine inspiration of the Holy Spirit, I broached a subject that I had never anticipated would ever surface in our conversations.

"David," I ventured further, my curiosity piqued, "might you be a member of the Freemasons?" His eyes widened slightly, a flicker of surprise crossing his face as if he had not anticipated the question. "Yes, indeed," he affirmed, a note of pride mingled with a hint of secrecy in his tone. "I'm a proud Freemason, following in the footsteps of my father and his father before him—a lineage steeped in Masonic tradition."

David then added, with a note of reverence, "My

beloved wife is an Eastern Star, a distinguished sisterhood within the grand tapestry of the Masonic order."

As we continued our conversations, we found ourselves at the crossroads of destiny, discussing the choices that define our paths. David shared the narrative of his life, his deeply held beliefs, and the principles that served as his compass. I listened intently, the vision still etched in my mind. Our discussions meandered through various subjects, including the concept of loyalty, particularly his allegiance to certain organizations that were interwoven with unique and unconventional perspectives. The depth of his convictions and the complexity of his affiliations added layers of deception, schemes, and intrigue to our dialogue, making it a conversation I would not soon forget.

In that instant, an air of self-assuredness swept across David's countenance, transforming it into a canvas of pride and satisfaction. "My granddaughters," he proclaimed with a sense of profound joy, "are active members of the young women's division of the esteemed institution, Job's Daughters." His words painted a vivid picture of a family deeply intertwined with the Masonic world.

My understanding of Freemasonry was not inconsequential; it was knowledge forged through research and the absorbing of stories from ex-members who had turned their backs on the fraternity, denouncing it as a clandestine cult with nefarious objectives—the worship and adoration of Satan and the "selling of one's soul" to him. With this knowledge at my disposal, I engaged him in a candid discourse, sharing the insights I had gleaned.

I explained the role of the "Worshipful Master," a revered position within the Masonic hierarchy, and the harrowing sacrifices required to ascend to such a level of authority—a pact sealed with the darkest forces.

The concept of "making a pact" or "selling one's soul" to the devil is a well-known phrase that refers to entering into a deal or compromise that contravenes and/or breaches one's moral values, beliefs, or principles. It often implies that an individual has made the decision to surrender their rights and submit to, worship, serve, and do the bidding of the devil, thus sacrificing their integrity in a desperate bid for personal gain, fame, success, and fortune.

Those who voluntarily enter such a covenant with the devil are often led and encouraged by human intermediaries, agents, or representatives who are themselves deeply entwined with the demonic realm and who guide or persuade others to follow suit.

The Root Cause of Evil is the Love of Money

The love of money is cited as the root cause of evil. This insatiable desire can lead individuals down a path of moral corruption, manifesting in various forms such as drug dealing, cheating, theft, human trafficking, and murder, to name just a few. These actions are driven by a deep-seated lust for wealth and power, ensnaring individuals in a web of temptation and vice.

As eloquently stated in Scripture, the pursuit of material gain can lead to one's downfall, highlighting the profound impact of greed on human behavior.

> *9 But they that will be rich fall into temptation and a snare, and into many foolish and hurtful lusts, which drown men in destruction and perdition.*
>
> *10 For the love of money is the root of all evil: which while some coveted after, they have erred from the faith, and pierced themselves through with many sorrows.*

> [11] *But thou, O man of God, flee these things; and follow after righteousness, godliness, faith, love, patience, meekness.*
>
> — 1 Timothy 6:9-11

To the Christian, the notion of selling one's soul is perceived as exchanging eternal salvation for transient, earthly gains and rewards. This act is regarded as a grave transgression, as it entails sacrificing one's spiritual integrity and relationship with God for temporary, worldly benefits.

The soul, being of divine origin, is beyond an individual's control or authority to sell or surrender. It is crucial to understand that no person holds the power to unreservedly yield their soul to the devil.

In addition, the soul is a divine gift from God and is not a commodity that can be bartered or traded. This misconception has led many down a treacherous path fraught with spiritual dangers and eternal repercussions. Our souls cannot be owned by the devil; they were created by God and therefore belong to Him.

Those who choose to make such a vow will find that the devil relentlessly pursues them to ensure they follow through. They will pay the highest price for their decision.

The following Scriptures reveal that Our Souls belong to God.

> [4] *Behold, all souls are mine; as the soul of the father, so also the soul of the son is mine: the soul that sinneth, it shall die.*
>
> — EZEKIEL 18:4

> [7] *And the Lord God formed man of the dust of the ground and breathed into his nostrils the breath of life; and man became a living soul.*
>
> — GENESIS 2:7

> [27] *What I tell you in darkness, that speak ye in light: and what ye hear in the ear, that preach ye upon the housetops.*
> [28] *And fear not them which kill the body, but are not able to kill the soul: but rather fear him which is able to destroy both soul and body in hell.*
>
> — MATTHEW 10:27-28

The Bible reveals that the god of this world, the devil, has blinded the minds of many, preventing them from hearing the truth. However, a day is coming when the voice of the devil, along with his threats and deceptions, will be silenced. He will receive his due reward, along with his cohorts and all those who chose to make him their god.

*4 In whom the god of this world hath blinded the minds of
them which believe not, lest the light of the glorious gospel
of Christ, who is the image of God, should shine unto
them. 5 For we preach not ourselves, but Christ Jesus the
Lord; and ourselves your servants for Jesus' sake. 6 For
God, who commanded the light to shine out of darkness,
hath shined in our hearts, to give the light of the
knowledge of the glory of God in the face of Jesus Christ.*

— 2 CORINTHIANS 4:4-6

10 And the devil that deceived them was cast into the lake of fire and brimstone, where the beast and the false prophet are, and shall be tormented day and night for ever and ever.

11 And I saw a great white throne, and him that sat on it, from whose face the earth and the heaven fled away; and there was found no place for them.

12 And I saw the dead, small and great, stand before God; and the books were opened: and another book was opened, which is the book of life: and the dead were judged out of those things which were written in the books, according to their works.

13 And the sea gave up the dead which were in it, and death and hell delivered up the dead which were in them: and they were judged every man according to their works.

14 And death and hell were cast into the lake of fire. This is the second death.

15 And whosoever was not found written in the book of life was cast into the lake of fire.

— REVELATION 20:10-15

The conflict facing humanity is profound, originating in the spiritual realm. The devil's ultimate goal is to divert human worship away from God and towards himself, enticing individuals and their families to make this misguided commitment in exchange for wealth, fame, and fortune, but it comes at a price! The spiritual battle requires us to be vigilant and steadfast in our faith. The following scriptures provide invaluable guidance on how we should position ourselves to resist temptation and avoid compromising our spiritual integrity.

> [11] *Put on the whole armour of God, that ye may be able to stand against the wiles of the devil.*
>
> [12] *For we wrestle not against flesh and blood, but against principalities, against powers, against the rulers of the darkness of this world, against spiritual wickedness in high places.*
>
> — EPHESIANS 6:11-12

> [8] *Be sober, be vigilant; because your adversary, the devil, as a roaring lion, walketh about, seeking whom he may devour.*
>
> — 1 PETER 5:8

The Holy Scriptures recount a profound event in which the devil endeavored to entice even Jesus into worshipping him. This occurred after Jesus had spent forty days in the wilderness, a narrative vividly depicted in Matthew 4:1-10.

In this passage, Jesus, after being baptized by John, is guided by the Holy Spirit into the wilderness—a place of desolation, solitude, and drought—to face temptation from the devil. After he fasted for forty days and nights, Jesus found himself physically weakened and hungry.

At this moment of vulnerability, the tempter approached Him and challenged Him, saying:

> [3] *If thou be the Son of God, command that these stones be made bread.*
>
> — MATTHEW 4:3

However, Jesus, with authority, answered:

> [4] *Man shall not live by bread alone, but by every word that proceedeth out of the mouth of God.*
>
> — MATTHEW 4:4

The devil, undeterred, took Jesus into the holy city and set Him on the pinnacle of the temple and said unto Him:

> [6] *If thou be the Son of God, cast thyself down: for it is written, He shall give His angels charge concerning thee: and in their hands they shall bear thee up, lest at any time thou dash thy foot against a stone.*
>
> — MATTHEW 4:6

Jesus countered with another verse of scripture and said unto him:

> *7 It is written again: thou shalt not tempt the Lord thy God.*
>
> — MATTHEW 4:7

In a final attempt, the devil took Jesus to an exceedingly high mountain, and showed Him all the kingdoms of the world and the glory of them; and said onto Him,

> *9 All these things will I give thee, if thou wilt fall down and worship me.*
>
> — MATTHEW 4:9

Jesus then said onto him:

> *10 Get thee hence, Satan: for it is written, Thou shalt worship the Lord thy God, and Him only shalt thou serve.*
>
> — MATTHEW 4:10

One of the key points here is, "All these things will I give thee, if thou wilt fall down and worship me." So, what does the devil want from you? Your worship! If you submit, he will give you the world, but at a price. It is a moral obligation for individuals worldwide to reject and sever any ties or associations with cults or activities that disrespect, dishonor, or blaspheme God's Holy Name. For God created all things, whether visible or invisible, and created them for His pleasure. God is the Creator of heaven and earth and everything therein. Therefore, it is essential to express sincere remorse and regret, seek His face in sincere repentance, denounce involvement in these cults, and earnestly seek His forgiveness.

The following scriptures reveal the immense power and authority of the Lord God, thus underscoring the folly and recklessness of worshipping the devil for fleeting, earthly gains.

> [16] *For by him were all things created, that are in heaven,*
> *and that are in earth, visible and invisible, whether they be*
> *thrones, or dominions, or principalities, or powers: all*
> *things were created by him, and for him:* [17] *And he is*
> *before all things, and by him, all things consist.*
>
> — COLOSSIANS 1:16-17

> [1] *In the beginning, God created the heaven and the earth.*
> [2] *And the earth was without form and void; and darkness*
> *was upon the face of the deep. And the Spirit of God*
> *moved upon the face of the waters.*
>
> — GENESIS 1:1-2

> [1] *Praise ye the Lord. Praise the Lord, O my soul.* [2] *While I*
> *live will I praise the Lord: I will sing praises unto my God*
> *while I have any being.* [3] *Put not your trust in princes,*
> *nor in the son of man, in whom there is no help.* [4] *His*
> *breath goeth forth, he returneth to his earth; in that very*
> *day, his thoughts perish.* [5] *Happy is he that hath the God*
> *of Jacob for his help, whose hope is in the Lord his God:*
> [6] *Which made heaven, and earth, the sea, and all that*
> *therein is: which keepeth truth for ever.*

— PSALM 146:1-6

[1] I will lift up mine eyes unto the hills, from whence cometh my help. [2] My help cometh from the Lord, which made heaven and earth.

— PSALM 121:1-2

[28] Hast thou not known? hast thou not heard, that the everlasting God, the Lord, the Creator of the ends of the earth, fainteth not, neither is weary? there is no searching of his understanding.

— ISAIAH 40:28

[18] For thus saith the Lord that created the heavens; God himself that formed the earth and made it; he hath established it, he created it not in vain, he formed it to be inhabited: I am the Lord; and there is none else.

— ISAIAH 45:18

[11] Thou art worthy, O Lord, to receive glory and honour and power: for thou hast created all things, and for thy pleasure they are and were created.

— REVELATION 4:11

[6] Thou, even thou, art Lord alone; thou hast made heaven, the heaven of heavens, with all their host, the earth, and all things that are therein, the seas, and all that is therein,

and thou preservest them all; and the host of heaven worshippeth thee.

— Nehemiah 9:6

[36] For what shall it profit a man, if he shall gain the whole world, and lose his own soul? [37] Or what shall a man give in exchange for his soul? [38] Whosoever therefore shall be ashamed of me and of my words in this adulterous and sinful generation; of him also shall the Son of man be ashamed, when he cometh in the glory of his Father with the holy angels.

— Mark 8:36-38

The devil's influence and deception have indeed left a lasting impact on human history. It was this devil, the embodiment of deceit, who beguiled Eve in the Garden of Eden, forever altering the course of mankind. Moreover, it was the same devil who masterminded the rebellion of one-third of heaven's angels against God.

[4] The Lord hath made all things for himself: yea, even the wicked for the day of evil.

— Proverbs 16:4

King Ahab, "A Sell-Out for the Devil"

The narrative of King Ahab and Naboth's vineyard, as chronicled in the biblical book of 1 Kings 21:20-25, is both intriguing and serves as a stark warning. King Ahab, a man ensnared in the web of his own greedy and covetous desires, had strayed from God's favor and tread the path of wickedness, mirroring the moral decay of Israel.

Ahab's eyes were set on Naboth's vineyard, a prized parcel of land that lay close to the royal palace. He desired to transform this space into a lush garden that would flourish with herbs. In his pursuit of this ambition, he proposed a trade to Naboth, offering him a superior vineyard elsewhere or a sum of money that equaled its value.

Naboth, a man of unwavering resolve, held his ground. The vineyard was more than mere property; it was his cherished inheritance, passed down through generations. It was a symbol of his family's history and their enduring connection to the land. It was not for sale, not at any price.

King Ahab, however, was consumed by a profound discontentment at Naboth's refusal to part with his land. A deep grief and sorrow gnawed at his heart, and in despair, he sought the company of his wife, Jezebel.

Jezebel, a fervent worshipper of Baal, a pagan deity, was known for her malevolent nature. She actively promoted the worship of Baal and Asherah, which was an abomination before God as it led to widespread idolatry in Israel. With her cunning mind and ruthless ambition, she devised a despicable scheme and made a solemn vow, a promise steeped in darkness, to secure the vineyard for Ahab at any cost. Her plan was one of treachery, deceit, and murder. The vineyard would be Ahab's, even if it meant staining their hands with innocent blood.

In the name of King Ahab. She penned letters, each one sealed with the royal insignia. These letters were dispatched to the city's respected pillars of society, the elders and nobles. The letters contained a series of sinister directives: to declare a fast and place Naboth on a pedestal among the people. Subsequently, they were to bring forth two men of ill repute, false witnesses, to bring grave accusations against Naboth, accusing him of blaspheming God and the king.

As the tragic narrative unfolded, the city's inhabitants, swayed and convinced by the deceptive words and the perceived authority of their leaders, led Naboth beyond the city walls. In a brutal act of mob justice, they pelted him with stones repeatedly until his life was extinguished, thus ending the life of an innocent man.

Upon receiving news of Naboth's demise, Jezebel wasted no time in urging Ahab to claim the vineyard, the very land that Naboth had held onto so tenaciously, refusing to trade it for money. With a chilling sense of triumph, she delivered the news to her husband, "Naboth is no longer among the living; he is dead."

Elijah, the revered prophet of the Lord, was a prophet during the reign of King Ahab. He is known for his zealous commitment to God and his role in challenging the worship of Baal and encouraging the worship of the True God.

One of Elijah's most notable acts was the confrontation with the prophets of Baal on Mount Carmel, where he demonstrated the power of God by calling down fire from heaven to consume the sacrifice to the Lord in 1 Kings 18.

With knowledge of Naboth's unjust murder by Ahab's wife, Jezebel, Elijah confronted King Ahab with a grave countenance. Ahab, caught off guard by the prophet's sudden appearance, exclaimed:

> [20] *Hast thou found me, O mine enemy?*
>
> — 1 KINGS 21:20

Elijah's voice, steady and resolute, answered:

> 20 *I have found thee, for thou hast sold thyself to work evil in the sight of the Lord.*
>
> — 1 KINGS 21:20

A chilling reflection of King Ahab's transgressions is chronicled in the annals of history, which is a reminder of the enduring impact of our choices.

> 25 *But there was none like unto Ahab, which did sell himself to work wickedness in the sight of the LORD, whom Jezebel, his wife, stirred up.*
>
> — 1 KINGS 21:25

~

The Captivating Mystique

Many individuals join Freemasonry for diverse reasons, including social interaction, networking opportunities, and philanthropic activities. It is not uncommon to find church leaders among the ranks of Masons. Historically, Freemasonry has had a presence in many churches and various religious institutions. It is important to note that Freemasonry has its origins in ancient pagan rituals. By taking an oath to this organization, individuals are, in essence, aligning themselves with a group that has controversial foundations, which is often perceived as a subsidiary or a mere front for a larger, more mysterious entity—the Illuminati.

Set Your House in Order

However, here I was, daring to breach the unspoken code of the Freemason brotherhood as I questioned David.

As the hours ebbed away, David and I shared our final words. With a heart full of sincerity and courage, I looked at him and said, "David, it's time for you to set your house in order." These words, new to my lips, were driven by a divine urgency. I was certain that the Spirit of the Lord was guiding me, for the message carried profound significance.

This situation draws an intriguing parallel to a biblical account in 2 Kings 20:1-6. King Hezekiah, gravely ill and facing his mortality, received a similar decree from the prophet Isaiah: [1]*Thus saith the LORD, set thine house in order; for thou shalt die, and not live.*

Hezekiah's response was deeply emotional—he turned to God in earnest prayer, and God, in His infinite mercy, granted him fifteen more years of life.

While I am by no means the prophet Isaiah, I felt a similar weight in my words to David; they carried both a warning and an opportunity—a chance for David to prepare, renounce any wrongdoings, and make peace with God.

In the charged silence, David's retort cut through the air like a razor-sharp blade: "End this conversation immediately," he commanded, "and never broach this topic with me again!" The forcefulness in his voice left no room for further negotiation or discussion. The gravity of his words lingered heavily in the air, even as our conversation came to a sudden and abrupt end.

I watched his car disappear into the night. The weight of his words lingered. A strange sense of sadness, infused with hope, filled my heart. I prayed that my warning would somehow reach him, that he would find the truth that had eluded him thus far.

In the solitude of my home, I reflected on the day's events. The vision of the flames, the voice of the Holy Spirit, and the revelation of David's ties to Freemasonry all swirled together. This experience, one of many in my journey of faith, would forever shape my understanding of the spiritual battles that rage unseen as the devil battles for the soul of every man, woman, and child.

A Transformation Unfolds

The ensuing months brought with them a refreshing change, a period of rejuvenation and anticipation. David embarked on a quest for purification, meticulously sorting through the clutter of his life with a steadfast determination to extricate himself from the influences that had long corrupted his heart. His resolve was like a beacon, guiding him through the murky fog of past misdeeds and casting a light on the path to redemption. He was making a concerted effort to rectify his wrongs, to cleanse himself of the ties that bound him to his past, and to separate himself from destructive influences.

But the allure of old habits and the seductive whispers of former associates proved too potent for his fledgling willpower. It was as if he stood at the edge of a precipice, the ground crumbling beneath his feet, and with a heart-wrenching inevitability, he succumbed. The enticement he once thought he could consume without consequence devoured him instead, and in a tragic reversal of roles, he transformed. I no longer had the ally I had cherished; he became the architect of my downfall, orchestrating a campaign of deceit, lies, and deception against me with one singular goal: to tarnish my reputation and sever my ties with the community I held dear, as well as with my religious and political acquaintances. The betrayal cut deep, leaving a wound that festered in the shadows of my trust.

One evening, as I was preparing for a board meeting where David and my fellow board members would be present, I was suddenly gripped by a compelling urge to remain at home. This thought sparked an internal struggle, as my sense of duty and responsibility vehemently beckoned me to fulfill my obligation to the meeting. Yet, as I stood by the front door, ready to step into the night, this overwhelming sensation lingered. In that moment of profound contemplation, I yielded and remained at home.

The pivotal board meeting occurred in my absence. In its aftermath, confusion reigned. The telephone rang, a chorus of concerned voices etching disbelief as anxious voices rang in my ears. "Why hadn't you informed us of your resignation?" they demanded. Their questions sliced through the air, sharp and unexpected, laden with a sense of betrayal, confusion, and unspoken accusations.

David, who was once the trusted confidant, wove a sinister web of deceit, portraying me as inadequate and lacking the expertise to fulfill my responsibilities. He crafted a narrative to vote me out, labeling me as unqualified and inexperienced for the role of Chair. He depicted me as an inept traitor in a tragic tale of my own downfall. His venomous words echoed through the boardroom, undermining my credibility and casting a shadow over my previously unblemished reputation.

"Don't worry about her," he said as he appeased the

unsuspecting board members, his voice a soothing balm on their concerns. "She won't be around too much longer." His words were shrouded in a sinister undertone. The chilling echo of his forecast hung in the air. His veiled threat, delivered with a disconcerting calm, left a cold, unsettling silence in its wake.

I could not help but wonder whether David was orchestrating my undoing and subsequent downfall. And what about my family, their safety, their peace of mind? Had I unsuspectingly stepped into a maze of danger?

In the days that followed, I found myself besieged by the relentless barrage of spiritual warfare. Night after night, sleep eluded me, and when slumber claimed me, it was a restless hostage to my anxieties. I would awaken, drenched in chilling perspiration, the echoes of my nightmares reverberating through the silence.

The attacks were merciless, a ceaseless onslaught that sought to chip away at my faith and determination. People began to distance themselves, their faces turning away in silent refusal to be linked with my plight. Most of the board, swayed by David's fabrications, aligned themselves against me. It was as if I were standing alone on a battlefield, the ground beneath me shaking with the force of their collective disbelief.

The sense of isolation was profound, starkly contrasting to the friendships that once prevailed. The trust that had been painstakingly built over the years seemed to crumble overnight, replaced by suspicion and doubt.

Betrayal lurked in every corner, even extending its reach to the verdant flora that adorned my office. The flowers and plants that graced my office, once vibrant and full of life, withered and wilted, succumbing to a mysterious disease, victims of an unseen poison. This enemy didn't just rob my plants of their vitality; the substance poured into my plants was colorless and odorless; it also suffocated me every time I set foot in my office.

Amidst this turbulence of adversity, my character became the battleground for a war I had not waged. Accusations, as venomous as they were unfounded, were hurled in my direction, each one a blow to the integrity I had spent a lifetime building. The charges were grave, the implications dire, and yet, I stood innocent, caught in the crossfire born from malice and deceit. I was to blame for uncovering and exposing their misdeeds.

I was constantly on my face in prayer, seeking God's protection and safety for my family and myself. The attacks targeted my job, my home, health, finances, and friendships. It had become intolerable.

When I sought the Lord in prayer in the wee hours of the morning, I would hear the repeated chirping of birds and the flapping of their wings right outside my bedroom window. When I investigated, there was nothing present.

After waking from sleep one morning around 2:30 a.m., I immediately rose from bed and knelt on the floor to pray. I was once again interrupted by the sound of fluttering wings and the chirping of birds outside my bedroom window. Unmoved, I remained in prayer. But I felt an urge within my spirit to look outside. Moving the curtain to one side and seeing nothing, I went back to pray.

But the fluttering of a bird's wing persisted. I peered out once more but saw nothing. Undeterred, I lingered by the window. My gaze drifted downwards, and there it was. Perched on a ledge a mere six feet below my window, a large white owl stood in all its majestic glory. I found myself questioning, "Why here?" It was a creature seemingly misplaced for that environment.

I released the curtain, my heart racing, and dashed into the other rooms. My sons, full of curiosity, followed. There it stood, unwavering—the White Snow Owl gazed directly at us, the three witnesses to this encounter. So often, I glimpsed curiosities, but rarely did others share those moments. Yet here, by the window, we stood united in this experience.

Snow Owls are natives of Alaska's cold vastness but not indigenous to New York. The thought reverberated in my mind—why this owl? And why now? I was acutely aware that owls, often revered as symbols of wisdom, have also been entwined with witchcraft across various cultures. I could not shake off the knowledge that my neighborhood was home to influential individuals who dabbled in the dark arts!

The owl's piercing gaze held mine. We stood there, frozen in silence. Then, in a sudden burst of emotion, the owl unfurled its wings and took flight, ascending into the night sky. We watched, taken aback, as the owl became a diminishing speck. Then, all at once, it was gone; it simply disappeared. I turned to look at my sons, their faces reflecting a mix of awe and wonder before we retreated to our own rooms.

The Beginning of the End

The spiritual attacks persisted relentlessly. A mere week had passed since David announced my impending departure. The news left me grappling with an unsettling feeling, a heavy burden weighing down my spirit. The emotional turmoil began to seep into my daily routine, compelling me to retire to bed earlier than usual.

At half past nine on a Tuesday evening, as I readied myself for bed, a sense of unease clung to me, refusing to dissipate. Overwhelmed, I found myself on my knees, seeking solace in prayer. Even as the words tumbled from my lips, the deep-seated trouble within me remained unshaken. Despite my fervent prayers, my spirit remained troubled.

That night, rest eluded me. The Spirit of God wanted my attention, so I continued in prayer. I found myself repenting; my soul laid bare. I also interceded for my family and asked the Lord to forgive them for any sins they might have committed. Down the list, I went—a prayer for grace and a plea for forgiveness.

The Lord, silent yet ever present, listened intently as I poured out my heart to Him. The room became my sanctuary, a haven of safety and whispered confessions. Returning to bed, I sought solace, and a slight peace settled over me, offering a fragile reprieve. However, the disturbing thoughts soon returned, more relentless than before. Once again, I found myself prostrate, crying out to God. I sensed something was amiss but could not discern what it was.

Hours passed as the battle raged with me. At 1:00 a.m., there was a shift—a weight lifted, and I felt free. The burdens of the soul dissolved. I climbed back into bed and fell asleep.

Later that morning, around 6:40 a.m., my cell phone rang. The caller ID displayed a name that took me by surprise—it was David! His call at such an hour was puzzling, especially considering the bitter words he had previously hurled in my direction. The air hung heavily with curiosity and a hint of trepidation.

The voice on the other end of the line was a tremor of raw grief, its intensity shattering the calm of the morning. "He's gone, Annette," the woman managed to choke out between sobs. "David is gone!" Her words hit me like a tidal wave.

"What do you mean he's gone?" I stammered, my voice barely above a whisper, quivering with shock and disbelief. "Who's gone?"

"David," she repeated, "my husband. He collapsed on the bathroom floor; I found him there… lifeless." Her voice broke as she continued, "The paramedics tried everything they could to revive him, but he… he just slipped away."

As her words sank in, a flood of memories washed over me. With his sharp wit and shrewd-like wisdom, David had once been a dear friend and confidant. However, over time, our friendship had become estranged, and he had become an adversary. His wife was unaware of the rift between us. Now, the news of his sudden departure left me grappling with a complex mix of emotions.

"I can't believe he's gone," her voice echoed through the phone line. "How am I going to live without him?" she cried. "I can't survive without him." Her sobs grew more intense, and she hung up, leaving my heart heavy.

David's passage into eternity, marked by the quiet hour of 1:00 a.m., left an indelible imprint on my soul. At 1:00 a.m. that morning, I sensed peace—instead of the ache that had clung to me and lodged in my chest. That heavy burden was lifted from my shoulders.

I lamented the loss of David and offered her my condolences and assistance in any way. But within, the question stirred: Could I have done more?

The Cavern of Hell

On an ordinary afternoon, just a few days following the devastating news of David's demise, I experienced another open vision. I was suspended or hovering in midair and found myself gazing into the foreboding caverns of hell, a realm of torment shrouded in oppressive gloom and impenetrable darkness.

And there, in that place, I caught a fleeting glimpse of David. Yet he remained oblivious to my presence, his attention ensnared by the grim surroundings. His form, etched with an eerie familiarity, maintained its usual silhouette. The contours of his figure and the structure of his frame all bore an uncanny resemblance to his physical manifestation in our world. It was as if he had been transported there in his corporal form, a chilling witness to the realism of this vision.

His face, a canvas of emotions, bore the confusion of a traveler who had taken a wrong turn. Disorientation reflected in his eyes, and disbelief etched deep lines. How had he arrived here, in this desolate place?

His gaze was drawn upward, captivated by the gaping jaws of the cavern in which he found himself standing. His thoughts, which I could clearly hear, echoed in the hollow silence—a desperate refrain reverberating with regret. "I wish I had listened to Annette; oh, how I wish I had listened to Annette and paid heed to her words."

In that moment suspended in time, I wrestled with the profound weight of decisions—the roads chosen and those left forsaken. Regrettably, my words to him had been cast aside and dismissed.

And so, I bore witness; I was unseen and unheard. His plea, a desperate cry for redemption, hung in the void, echoing off the cavern walls unanswered. A wave of sorrow washed over me for my old friend, caught in the throes of his own choices.

I am reminded of another vivid open vision that unfolded several years earlier. In this vision, I beheld a well-known international figure in the depths of hell. His arrival was marked by a resounding "thud" as his feet contacted the ground, causing a cloud of dust to rise from the dry, dirty gray earth. He was clad in a black suit, white shirt, and what appeared to be a black tie. His presence exuded an eerie intensity, leaving an indelible impression on my soul.

As he landed, the figure began to fumble with his tie, his hand trembling slightly, betraying his outward composure. His gaze drifted upward, taking in the horrifying spectacle around him—the flames, the tortured souls, and the oppressive darkness. A slight disdain, tinged with fear and disbelief, was etched across his face, a chilling realization of his grim fate and the stark reality of hell. His eyes darted wide with terror as he tried to make sense of the nightmarish scene before him.

In the deafening silence of the moment, I heard his thoughts. He was trying to summon the courage to voice the question that gnawed at his mind, a desperate plea for understanding in the face of the inexplicable. "Why am I here?" he wondered, his confusion and fear intertwining in a silent scream that echoed through the fiery abyss. His mind raced, searching for answers but finding only the oppressive weight of his eternal punishment.

Is "Hell" a real place?

The question of whether Hell is a real place has been the topic of frequent discussion and debate. Based on my understanding and belief, I assert that it indeed exists. This belief is not unfounded; it is substantiated by numerous references found within Scripture, where Hell is explicitly and unequivocally mentioned.

> [16] *The Lord is known by the judgment which he executeth: the wicked is snared in the work of his own hands. Higgaion. Selah.* [17] *The wicked shall be turned into hell, and all the nations that forget God.*
>
> — PSALM 9:16-17

> [24] *The way of life is above to the wise, that he may depart from hell beneath.*
>
> — PROVERBS 15:24:

Indeed, even the Lord Himself, in His profound teachings, has referred to Hell as a tangible realm of torment and despair:

> [28] *And fear not them which kill the body, but are not able to kill the soul: but rather fear him which is able to destroy both soul and body in hell.*
>
> — MATTHEW 10:28

> [42] *And shall cast them into a furnace of fire: there shall be wailing and gnashing of teeth.*
>
> [50] *And shall cast them into the furnace of fire: there shall be wailing and gnashing of teeth.*
>
> — MATTHEW 13:42, 50

> 41 *Then shall he say also unto them on the left hand, Depart from me, ye cursed, into everlasting fire, prepared for the devil and his angels:*
>
> — MATTHEW 25:41

> 43 *And if thy hand offend thee, cut it off: it is better for thee to enter into life maimed, than having two hands to go into hell, into the fire that never shall be quenched:* 44 *Where their worm dieth not, and the fire is not quenched.* 45 *And if thy foot offend thee, cut it off: it is better for thee to enter halt into life, than having two feet to be cast into hell, into the fire that never shall be quenched:* 46 *Where their worm dieth not, and the fire is not quenched.*
>
> 47 *And if thine eye offend thee, pluck it out: it is better for thee to enter into the kingdom of God with one eye, than having two eyes to be cast into hell fire:* 48 *Where their worm dieth not, and the fire is not quenched.*
>
> — MARK 9:43-48

> 4 *For if God spared not the angels that sinned, but cast them down to hell, and delivered them into chains of darkness, to be reserved unto judgment;*
>
> — 2 PETER 2:4

The Lake of Fire, which is the final death, where death and hell will be cast into it, represents the final judgment: Revelation 14,15, Revelation 19:20, Revelation 20:10-14, and Revelation 21:8.

Hell is not a destination assigned arbitrarily or capriciously. It is not a fate imposed without choice or consent. Rather, it is a path that individuals consciously choose to tread—a consequence of decisions made in the exercise of free will. It is the result of a series of choices that lead away from the light and into the darkness. The Lord, in His infinite wisdom and boundless love, desires for all of us to choose life—to choose Him.

Numerous individuals have recounted their chilling encounters with the terrifying aspects of the underworld during episodes of near-death experiences, as well as through dreams and visions. These narratives often depict a realm filled with unspeakable dread, reinforcing the concept of hell as a place of ongoing torment.

God's love for the world is immeasurable. He made a way for humanity to be reconciled to Himself by sending His only begotten Son, the Lord Jesus Christ. Jesus took upon Himself the sins of the world so that we might not perish and be banished to hell but have eternal life with the Father and His Son in Heaven. God did not send His Son into the world to condemn it but that the world through Him might be saved. This profound truth is beautifully expressed in the following Scripture:

> 16 *For God so loved the world, that he gave his only begotten Son, that whosoever believeth in him should not perish but have everlasting life.* 17 *For God sent not his Son into the world to condemn the world, but that the world through him might be saved.*
>
> 18 *He that believeth on him is not condemned: but he that believeth not is condemned already, because he hath not believed in the name of the only begotten Son of God."*
>
> 19 *And this is the condemnation, that light is come into*

the world, and men loved darkness rather than light because their deeds were evil. [20] *For everyone that doeth evil hateth the light, neither cometh to the light, lest his deeds should be reproved.* [21] *But he that doeth truth cometh to the light, that his deeds may be made manifest, that they are wrought in God.*

— JOHN 3:16-21

It is God's desire that all people receive His salvation by first repenting and turning away from their sins. The Scripture in 2 Peter 3:9 provides a comforting reassurance:

[9] *The Lord is not slack concerning his promise, as some men count slackness; but is longsuffering to us-ward, not willing that any should perish, but that all should come to repentance.*

As such, every individual is granted freedom of choice. This choice, then, becomes a pivotal factor in determining one's spiritual journey and ultimate destination.

The Final Culmination

In the solemn week that followed David's passing, the world seemed to stand still. It was during this time of reflection and mourning that I received a call that would stir the still waters of my soul. The voice at the other end was one of comfort and authority, belonging to a dear friend who walked in the dual anointing of a prophet and an apostle.

His words were like balm to my aching heart, infused with encouragement and divine purpose. He shared with me a revelation that, amidst his fervent prayers, my name surfaced, prompting him to reach out and deliver a message of encouragement to me.

I requested approximately ten minutes to deliver a package and took a brief moment to collect my thoughts. I assured him that I would return his call shortly.

When the time arrived to reconnect, his greeting was nothing short of miraculous. "Oh my God," he exclaimed, his voice tinged with awe, "you'll never believe what just happened! I was driving, and the worship music turned up high, when suddenly, I heard the voice of the Lord. It was clear, cutting through the melody with an instruction that could not be ignored: *"TURN OFF THE MUSIC,"* the voice said, *"YOU'RE ABOUT TO GET A CALL."* His heart, filled with understanding, knew this was a moment of divine guidance and instruction.

Obediently, he silenced the tunes that filled his car, and in that very instant, his cell phone came to life. The caller ID displayed my name, confirming the divine appointment that had been made.

This encounter, so small yet so profound, served as a reminder that in our moments of deepest need, we are never alone. The Lord orchestrates our steps, aligns our paths, and speaks into the harshness of life to reach us with His perfect timing.

I confided in my friend about the events that preceded David's death. A mere week before his passing, he had sown seeds of discord among the board, casting shadows of doubt over my future involvement. His words, like frightening premonitions, hinted at an end for me that seemed undeserved. My friend listened intently as I continued.

The tale I recounted grew darker as I spoke of an

incident a month prior. Two board members who once stood by my side had turned against me. Their words, laced with malice, sought to undermine my authority, instructing the staff to defy my directives. The rebellion they incited was a poison, spreading through the ranks and threatening the very foundation of our collective mission.

One morning in the office, a high-ranking colleague approached me with a menacing glare. She invaded my personal space, jabbing her finger inches from my face, and furiously shouted, "You're going down!" Unfazed, I stood firm and, without flinching, demanded, "Remove your finger from my face." In an instant, the rest of the office staff rallied around her, visibly showing their support.

The situation demanded intervention, and amidst the turmoil, a lone ally emerged. One board member, whose loyalty remained unshaken, reached out to the public official responsible for our appointments as commissioners. An emergency meeting was convened, a gathering that would set the stage for a confrontation between truth and betrayal.

As the Board and staff assembled, the public official's voice rang clear, affirming my leadership and the necessity of adherence to my directives. His ultimatum was unequivocal: those who opposed the established order were free to resign from their positions. It was a moment of reckoning, a line drawn in the sand that would reveal the hearts of all who had assembled.

Amidst the tension, a board member arose, her gaze fixed directly upon me with intent. In a brazen display of defiance, she sought to invoke a curse upon me and my children.

Yet, as her words hung in the air, I felt a righteous indignation. With unwavering conviction, I faced her and pronounced, "I reverse that curse in the Name of Jesus!" It was a declaration of faith and a testament to the power vested in us to overcome darkness with light.

In the wake of that encounter, tragedy struck. The nephew of the cursing board member met an untimely end one week after her outburst despite a successful surgery.

The other conspirator, who had whispered lies concerning me into the ears of officials, was struck down by a massive stroke that left her unable to speak. She had no choice but to resign from the board.

These events, though sorrowful, served as a reminder of the consequences that befall those who wield hatred and wickedness.

My friend listened intently to my account, his silence a canvas for contemplation. Then, with sudden clarity, he spoke the word of the Lord: "The demons of this city have convened and assembled in fear, for they recognize the might of our God, the Creator of Heaven and Earth. Their schemes, plans, and structures are in disarray, disorder, and confusion. Their weapons of warfare have been rendered futile and ineffective. Take heart, for the Lord God, the Creator of Heaven and Earth, is protecting you, for His hand is upon your life!"

If you find yourself in a place of compromise and sin, having made wrong choices, please reflect upon the following heartfelt prayer inspired by the Psalms, followed by the Prayer of Repentance and Renunciation. This prayer draws from a Psalm of David, written after he committed adultery with Bathsheba, the wife of Uriah the Hittite, and impregnated her. To conceal his sin, David arranged to have

Uriah to be placed at the forefront of the hottest battle, ensuring his death. Refer to 2 Samuel 11, 12, & 1 Kings 1, 2.

PRAYER

> *1 Have mercy upon me, O God, according to thy lovingkindness: according unto the multitude of thy tender mercies blot out my transgressions. 2 Wash me thoroughly from my iniquity, and cleanse me from my sin. 3 For I acknowledge my transgressions: and my sin is ever before me. 4 Against thee, thee only, have I sinned, and done this evil in thy sight: that thou mightest be justified when thou speakest, and be clear when thou judgest. 5 Behold, I was shapen in iniquity; and in sin did my mother conceive me. 6 Behold, thou desirest truth in the inward parts: and in the hidden part thou shalt make me to know wisdom. 7 Purge me with hyssop, and I shall be clean: wash me, and I shall be whiter than snow. 8 Make me to hear joy and gladness; that the bones which thou hast broken may rejoice. 9 Hide thy face from my sins, and blot out all mine iniquities. 10 Create in me a clean heart, O God; and renew a right spirit within me. 11 Cast me not away from thy presence; and take not thy holy spirit from me. 12 Restore unto me the joy of thy salvation; and uphold me with thy free spirit. 13 Then will I teach transgressors thy ways; and sinners shall be converted unto thee. 14 Deliver me from bloodguiltiness, O God, thou God of my salvation: and my tongue shall sing aloud of thy righteousness. 15 O Lord, open thou my lips; and my mouth shall shew forth thy praise.*
>
> — PSALM 51:1-15 (KING JAMES VERSION)

1 O loving and kind God, have mercy. Have pity upon me and take away the awful stain of my transgressions. 2 Oh, wash me, cleanse me from this guilt. Let me be pure again. 3 For I admit my shameful deed—it haunts me day and night. 4 It is against you and you alone I sinned and did this terrible thing. You saw it all, and your sentence against me is just. 5 But I was born a sinner, yes, from the moment my mother conceived me. 6 You deserve honesty from the heart; yes, utter sincerity and truthfulness. Oh, give me this wisdom. 7 Sprinkle me with the cleansing blood[a and I shall be clean again. Wash me and I shall be whiter than snow. 8 And after you have punished me, give me back my joy again. 9 Don't keep looking at my sins—erase them from your sight. 10 Create in me a new, clean heart, O God, filled with clean thoughts and right desires. 11 Don't toss me aside, banished forever from your presence. Don't take your Holy Spirit from me. 12 Restore to me again the joy of your salvation, and make me willing to obey you. 13 Then I will teach your ways to other sinners, and they—guilty like me—will repent and return to you. 14-15 Don't sentence me to death. O my God, you alone can rescue me. Then I will sing of your forgiveness, [b] for my lips will be unsealed—oh, how I will praise you.

— Psalm 51:1-15 (The Living Bible)

18 Come now, and let us reason together, saith the Lord: though your sins be as scarlet, they shall be as white as snow; though they be red like crimson, they shall be as wool.

— Isaiah 1:18

PRAYER OF REPENTANCE AND RENUNCIATION

Heavenly Father,

I humbly come before You with a contrite heart, seeking Your forgiveness and cleansing from all my sins. I acknowledge my failings, weaknesses, and the moments when I strayed from Your righteous path. I repent and renounce any alliances or compromises that do not align with Your divine Will.

I specifically renounce my involvement and participation in any cult organization, including [name the organization] and/or religious groups that do not represent You, honor You, or align with Your divine Will and purpose for my life. I break free from any entanglements that hinder my relationship with You and denounce my involvement in organizations that worship the devil. I acknowledge and agree that these actions and associations are an abomination in Your sight.

I surrender my desires, my fears, and my doubts to You. I ask that You cleanse me from all unrighteousness and guide me back to Your truth and righteousness. Father, I pray that Your goodness and mercy will follow me all the days of my life, so that I may dwell in Your House forever. (Psalm 23).

For it is in Jesus' Name, I pray. Amen.

Chapter 2

Devil On Assignment

We sat for a moment in a secluded area of the parking lot, our vehicle filled to the brim with the remnants of a day spent in a laborious transition. The overstuffed seats cradled our tired bodies, offering a moment of respite from the chaos.

As the afternoon wore on, we noticed the striking landscape and flower beds scattered across the campus. These details did not reveal themselves all at once; rather, they unfolded like a story as we sat and talked, pointing out areas that caught our attention. With each passing moment, we became increasingly impressed by the natural beauty that the university had to offer.

Trees of all shapes and sizes towered over us, standing as silent sentinels against the magnificent backdrop that discreetly concealed a handful of residential structures. These buildings, each boasting eclectic architecture, added to the rich tapestry of the vast campus grounds. The university was steeped in history and boasted robust graduate and undergraduate programs, with the music program being no exception.

Taking solace in the brief interval, we watched the sky gradually surrender its light, painting a canvas of deepening blues and purples around us.

Despite the energy we had expended over the past few hours, it had become essential to pause and rejuvenate our spirits from the arduous task of cleaning and the hauling of crammed boxes.

These boxes, filled with the tangible pieces of my daughter's life, were now making their journey to her new dorm room, nestled on the fourth floor of the student housing complex.

When we arrived on the university grounds earlier that morning, we were greeted by the serendipity of securing a convenient parking spot. It was mercy that spared us from the intense frustration and chaotic movement that often accompanies such significant life events. But once inside the actual building, we joined the bustling throng of first-year students, parents, and friends. Each of us shared a common purpose: to set up a home away from home for our loved ones in their respective dorm rooms.

My daughter applied to this prestigious university with the aspiration of being accepted into their esteemed vocal performance program. From an early age, she had nurtured a profound passion for music and harbored a dream of becoming a professional singing artist dedicated to the Lord.

She was captivated by the diversity and exceptional talent of the other applicants, who hailed from various corners of the globe and brought with them a rich tapestry of musical backgrounds and styles. This exposure further fueled her desire to delve into specific genres of music, starting with jazz, classical, and opera. She was determined to uncover the yet undiscovered facets of her vocal artistry.

Several years later, this journey of discovery culminated in her securing a vocal role in the historic opera *Porgy and Bess*. Her participation in this renowned production afforded her the remarkable opportunity to travel nationally with the company, showcasing her talent on a grand stage.

We learned that only a select number of students are accepted annually into this prestigious university and awarded full scholarships. After spending one year at a local college with a smaller student body, my daughter made the pivotal decision to transfer to this esteemed institution, hoping that she was on the right path to achieving her dream.

The journey was far from easy. It involved months of intense interviews, a deluge of paperwork, and a rigorous audition period under the scrutiny of a group of perceptive adjudicators. Despite the challenges, she remained steadfast and determined. She received the decision she had been eagerly awaiting. Unable to contain her excitement, she learned that she had been accepted and awarded not one but two full scholarships, along with a partial housing grant.

My daughter was overjoyed by this incredible opportunity and felt ready to face any challenge and seize every possibility that lay ahead. Remarkably, everything seemed to fall effortlessly into place, and she embraced this new chapter with unwavering enthusiasm and gratitude.

But the day my daughter received her acceptance letter, everything changed. A cold shiver ran down my spine, and I felt an overwhelming sense that something was terribly wrong. She looked at me, expecting to see joy and excitement, but I found it difficult to embrace the news with the same enthusiasm. Instead, I was consumed by a surge of concern.

For months leading up to this moment, I had been sensing an uneasiness regarding the university. Despite my efforts to express my concerns to my daughter and mother, I struggled to articulate the reasons behind my hesitations. Thankfully, my family has come to understand me better over time. They know that when I sense something might be amiss, even if I don't have the full revelation or understanding right away, it is wise to wait it out with me. Seldom am I wrong in these matters.

I conveyed to them that I sensed something was not as it should be, though I could not pinpoint exactly what it was. Deep down, I harbored the hope that she would consider applying elsewhere. My failure at the time was not being forthright with my mother and daughter from the beginning. Instead, I kept those emotions concealed within me, like an old wineskin on the verge of imploding.

As the months rapidly progressed toward the September start date, my sense of trepidation grew stronger. It was a feeling I could not shake, a persistent whisper of doubt that lingered in the back of my mind. Despite my reservations, I recognized that this was a pivotal moment in my daughter's life, a crucial steppingstone toward her future successes.

As my conviction intensified, I knew I had to confront the unease that had taken root in my heart. I needed to approach my daughter and mother to share the turmoil that churned within me. Yet, once again, I found myself without a compelling reason to explain why I felt she should not attend the university. I also sensed that the precious Holy Spirit was seeking my attention, and I understood the importance of being patient and prayerful until His message was revealed.

My daughter's dorm room was on the fourth floor of the four-story student housing complex, which was divided by gender. The first floor was reserved exclusively for male students, while the second and third floors were unisex. The fourth floor, where we now stood, was designated for female students only.

Upon entering her room, we met her roommate, a petite and pleasant first-year student who had already claimed the only single bed in the room, having arrived earlier that morning. My daughter, gracious and adaptable, surveyed the room. Her eyes settled on the bottom bunk of the two-tier metal bunk bed positioned on the opposite side of the room.

The furnishings in the dorm room were sparse: two beds, two storage wardrobes, and a separate closet for clothes and other personal belongings. One large desk, designed to accommodate two individuals simultaneously, was also present. Two oversized windows flanked either side of the room, providing an ample amount of natural light.

Together, my mother, daughter, and I spent several hours meticulously cleaning and sanitizing every surface within reach. Our overzealousness meant that long after the other students had finished setting up and begun to relax, we were still ascending the four flights of stairs, arms laden with boxes, to her dorm room.

By 9:30 pm, we were completely exhausted and famished, having worked continuously for hours with very few breaks. We decided to leave the campus in search of sustenance, our bodies crying out for rest and our minds weighed down by the day's events.

As we drove away from the university, the city lights began to twinkle in the distance, and the cool night air brushed against our faces through the open car windows. My daughter, on the cusp of a new chapter in her life, seemed contemplative, considering the future that lay ahead. My mother, ever the pillar of strength, appeared reflective, her eyes gazing out into the night as if seeking answers to unspoken questions.

And then there was me, caught in the grip of an internal struggle, wrestling with a sense of foreboding that refused to be ignored despite the joyous occasion. It was as if a gentle whisper from the Holy Spirit was trying to guide me, to warn me of something yet unseen. I prayed silently for clarity, for the courage to voice my concerns, and for the wisdom to discern the path that lay before us.

The restaurant we chose was a quaint little diner. We settled into a cozy booth and allowed ourselves to finally relax. The aroma of freshly brewed coffee and the sound of soft music in the background provided a soothing backdrop to our meal. As we ate, we spoke of the day's events, future plans, and the hopes and dreams that filled our hearts.

It was there, at that diner, that I finally found the strength to voice what was in my heart. I shared with my daughter and mother the deep-seated concerns that had been troubling me, the sense of unease that had been my constant companion in the months leading up to this day. I spoke of the Holy Spirit's prompting, emphasizing the need to be vigilant and prayerful as we navigated this new journey.

My daughter listened intently, her eyes reflecting maturity beyond her years. She understood the weight of my words and the love that fueled them. My mother, too, offered her unwavering support, reminding us that our faith in God and the guidance of the Holy Spirit would lead us through any uncertainty. Together, we found solace in our shared faith, knowing that we were never truly alone and that God's presence was with us.

As we left the diner and before making our way back to the university, we noticed that the night seemed a little less dark, the stars a little brighter. We sat in the vehicle for a while and prayed; this is what we knew to do—to talk to our Heavenly Father in prayer for complete guidance, direction, and revelation, trusting that He would make known to us what we needed to see and understand more clearly.

Back on Campus

We headed back to the campus with renewed spirits, ready to face whatever challenges lay ahead. Once there, I grabbed a box from the back of the vehicle and entered the building while my mother and daughter remained in the vehicle conversing. But upon entering the enclosed stairwell, I paused.

Standing motionless at the foot of the stairwell, the decision to ascend weighed heavily upon me, not knowing whether this would become a "fight or flight" situation. The day had been long, and the countless trips up and down the enclosed space had become a monotonous undertaking. Yet, this time was different; a palpable shift in the atmosphere halted me in my tracks. I was acutely aware that something was amiss, a feeling that gnawed at the edges of my consciousness, urging me to take heed.

There are moments in life that carve themselves into memory, indelible and disturbing. As I climbed higher, each step seemed to amplify my discomfort, a crescendo of unease that I could not ignore. I knew, with a certainty that defied logic, that something was terribly wrong.

> [8] *Be sober, be vigilant; because your adversary the devil, as a roaring lion, walketh about, seeking whom he may devour.*
>
> — 1 PETER 5:8

Approaching the second-floor landing, I moved with extreme caution, my senses heightened to the eerie stillness that enveloped me. An abrupt sensation washed over me, a chilling awareness of an unclean and malevolent presence. Though my eyes saw nothing, and my ears heard only silence, the voice of the Holy Spirit was a Comforter, reminding me of the authority bestowed upon us in Jesus' name.

No one else entered the stairwell; still, it felt as though the very air was thick with a deep hush. As I arrived at the third-floor landing, my gaze was inexplicably drawn to a particular corner where two walls converged. Standing rigid with its back against the wall was a bulky, dark gray, shadowy figure.

My mind struggled to comprehend the sight before me —a hideous demonic spirit from the depths of hell itself. I was aware that I was seeing into the spirit realm. We were acutely aware of each other, and for a fleeting moment, our eyes met in a silent acknowledgment of the other's presence. Its eyes, deep-set and as dark as the void, shifted away from mine, darting from side to side, then down to the ground, as if to avoid my scrutiny. It was perceived that I knew why it was there. Strangely, it appeared fierce but displayed an apprehension concerning me.

> [1]*And when he had called unto him his twelve disciples, he gave them power against unclean spirits, to cast them out, and to heal all manner of sickness and all manner of disease.*
>
> — MATTHEW 10:1

In that moment, as surreal as it may sound, I was acutely aware of my surroundings, which were enveloped by a profound sense of calm. No fear took hold of me; I was utterly unafraid. Yet within me, a flame of hope flickered, fueled by the unwavering protection of the Lord's angels. I knew I was not alone. It was a certainty beyond doubt that God's presence and protection were wrapped around me, a shield against the darkness that loomed before me.

As the revelation unfolded, I understood that its only purpose in this world was to bring injury and destruction, a hideous existence indeed. What awaits it and the devil whom it serves and obeys is eternity in the Lake of Fire. It already knows what looms ahead.

This spirit was larger than the average person, adorned in a seamless dark-gray garment that covered its entire body. Through the revelation of the Spirit of God, I suddenly realized that I was witnessing a violent and destructive entity of "rape." The Holy Spirit assured me that this malevolent spirit could not harm me, for His holy angels were protecting me. Deep within, I sensed that its true purpose was to bring harm to my daughter, which clarified my strong opposition to this university.

Additionally, the Holy Spirit revealed that this wicked spirit was dispatched from the very pits of hell on a devastating assignment to wreak havoc on lives and cause physical and emotional harm.

Rape is an unlawful sexual activity carried out forcibly or under threat or injury against a person's will." (Merriam-Webster Dictionary). The aftermath of rape leaves its victim devasted and demoralized.

I became aware of the method by which the destruction would unfurl its malicious wings. A time was approaching when this ravenous evil spirit would execute its destructive plan. It would remain hidden in the shadows of the dimly lit staircase, the very spot where my eyes had glimpsed it. Its purpose, vile and dormant, was to simply wait. Then, an unsuspecting vessel would ascend those stairs—a weak human vessel. This vessel was not weak physically but lacked self-control, self-discipline, and strength of mind. The evil spirit would latch itself onto the human vessel. Once attached, it would use this vessel as an instrument of darkness to carry out the intended evil act, leaving behind a trail of devastation and suffering.

I reflected on how evilness thrives in the shadows, where it is least expected.

With a steadiness that belied the situation, I continued my ascent, each step an act of faith. I clung to the knowledge and comfort that I was not alone, that the Holy Spirit was my constant companion, and that the holy angels of God were protecting me through this trial.

The evil spirit remained motionless, a silent sentinel that watched as I passed by, its presence a dismal reminder of the spiritual battles that raged unseen. Upon reaching my daughter's dorm room, I sat down on her bed with a sense of relief. The encounter in the stairwell lingered in my mind. This was a clear reminder that our struggles are not against flesh and blood but against the rulers, against the authorities, against the powers of this dark world, and against the spiritual forces of evil in the heavenly realms.

> *[11] Put on the whole armour of God, that ye may be able to stand against the wiles of the devil. [12] For we wrestle not against flesh and blood, but against principalities, against powers, against the rulers of the darkness of this world, against spiritual wickedness in high places.*
>
> — Ephesians 6:11-12

As I rejoined my mother and daughter in the car, I shared with them the profound experience I had just encountered and the assurance of God's unwavering protection. We prayed together, giving heartfelt thanks to Almighty God for His divine intervention and safeguarding my daughter and the other students. We sought the Lord's wisdom for the days ahead, trusting in His guidance.

The experience in the stairwell became a defining moment that resonated deeply with us throughout the following months. We continued to pray for my daughter and the entire student body at the campus, fervently hoping that the troubling vision I had witnessed would not come to pass. Although my daughter was initially pleased to have been accepted by the university, she later confided that this was not the place God had intended for her to complete her education.

Challenging Campus Experience

After three months on campus, my daughter began experiencing serious issues with her roommate and another fellow student, which significantly impacted her well-being and academic performance. Her roommate would frequently bring different young men into their room at night, assuming my daughter was asleep, and engage in intimate activities with them. This occurred multiple times per week, making my daughter feel uncomfortable, unsafe, and violated in her own living space.

Moreover, she noticed unsettling activities on campus, including being followed by a mysterious man who was also a student at the university. His nails were painted black, and he never made eye contact with her but appeared to be stalking her, always showing up wherever she went, such as the computer lab, the bus stop, or the library. He never spoke to her but would sit closely behind her, and she would catch him staring at her when she turned her head slightly. This made her feel anxious and uneasy. These incidents were affecting her physically and emotionally, compromising her safety and security on campus.

Some of the students belonged to a secret coven and were surprised when she showed no interest in joining their "club" despite being invited numerous times. Additionally, the constant playing of loud rock music from the floors below hers disrupted her dorm room study time, affecting her focus and energy.

Seeking refuge in the library to study at night after classes became unappealing due to the sudden disappearance of stray cats on campus. These feral cats roamed freely, but some were found decapitated on the campus grounds the following morning. Walking from the library to her dorm room at night made her uncomfortable.

My daughter had become lethargic and could no longer manage the demands placed on her. She was being pulled in every direction except the right one, and her grades began to suffer terribly. While friends skipped classes due to hangovers from the night before, she would stay up all night studying but still struggled to grasp her studies. This was highly unusual for a bright and studious individual.

The two music scholarships did not come through, and the partial housing grant was also pulled. She was becoming increasingly stressed. On Fridays, I would drive to campus and bring her home for the weekend so she could get some peace of mind. But by Sunday night, she was back on campus.

Her mental well-being was severely challenged, and she slept for hours at a time. She had no energy, no strength, and lacked willpower. She was failing in every subject. It was then that I made the difficult decision to withdraw her from the university.

The Dark Descent

But the day arrived when the word of knowledge that was revealed to me in the stairwell unfolded precisely as foretold. A young man stepped onto university grounds; his presence marked by an eerie vulnerability—the very weakness the Holy Spirit warned me about. As he entered the enclosed stairwell and ascended the stairs, the evil spirit, sensing its moment, lunged from its concealed lair and clung to him, its dark intent driving it to orchestrate the sinister act that awaited.

He ran up the remaining stairs and burst into the women's showers. The lone female student must have stood frozen under the water, her eyes wide with shock. She had no chance to react before he lunged at her. Her screams went unheard because the other students were in their classrooms in another building. They were oblivious to the horror unfolding in the student housing facility on the fourth floor in the women's bathroom. Fueled by the demonic force that drove him, he attacked the young woman, and when he was done, he fled—retracing his steps down the stairs of the enclosed stairwell and out of the building and vanished. The female student lay broken and violated, her life forever altered by the evil that had descended upon her.

A Twist of Fate

The morning of the attack unfolded like any other—my daughter, now withdrawn from the university, would have taken her shower at the exact hour the young woman had taken hers. But in the aftermath, questions lingered, and chaos ensued. The campus, once a sanctuary of learning, had become one of urgency and high tension and the focal point of a significant incident. Before long, the air was filled with the thumping rotors of helicopters hovering overhead, each one carrying trained observers scanning the ground below.

Police vehicles, marked and unmarked, cordoned off the area, their lights casting an uncanny glow against the backdrop of the academic edifices. With cameras and microphones ready, news media personnel were stationed at strategic points, eager to capture the unfolding events and relay them to a captivated audience. And amidst the tension, the paramedics stood with their kits meticulously organized and prepared for any eventuality. Their presence was a stark reminder of the potential for tragedy at any moment.

The investigations were thorough and relentless, stretching over several days. Detectives and forensic teams worked tirelessly, combing through evidence, interviewing the victim and potential witnesses, and piecing together the sequence of events that led to the crisis. Understandably, the campus community was on edge, the atmosphere heavy with anticipation and concern.

Finally, after days of relentless pursuit, a crucial breakthrough emerged. An inconspicuous figure—a delivery driver, not a student—who had made several deliveries at the university in the past but had previously gone unnoticed amidst the sea of faces was revealed. Once overlooked, his presence became the focal point of the investigation, shedding light on the mystery that had gripped the campus. He had managed to slip through the cracks and was later identified and apprehended.

The arrest marked the end of the immediate chaos, but it was just the beginning of a long journey for justice and understanding. The young man's fate, a fragile strand in this unfolding drama, now rested in the hands of the justice system. As a vessel of choices and consequences, he awaits his reckoning.

As for the victim, time stretches before us—an expanse where wounds may mend, and hearts may find comfort. It is my prayer that her need for healing will be met swiftly.

PRAYER FOR THE VICTIM

Dear Heavenly Father,

Today, I lift up to You the victims of crimes who find themselves ensnared in the throes of undeserved and unwarranted attacks. Grant them the strength and support of compassionate individuals to help them piece together the shattered fragments of their lives. Guide them toward counseling and resources that will aid in their recovery from trauma.

I ask that You help them refrain from self-blame and let this setback propel them toward a future filled with positivity and impact, enabling them to assist others in similar situations. Surround them with caring, loving, and understanding individuals who recognize their sensitivity and vulnerability. May they seek and find healing and restoration in every aspect of their lives. Grant them the grace to forgive and move forward.

We ask this petition in Jesus' name. Amen.

PRAYER FOR THE ASSAILANT/ ATTACKER/ AGGRESSOR

Dear Heavenly Father,

It is a sorrowful day for those who are vulnerable, uncontrollable, and tormented by hate. Open their eyes to the error of their ways and guide them toward the help and counseling they so desperately need to prevent the repetition of their misdeeds. Place them in environments where assistance is readily available.

I pray for the healing of their minds and that they may be made whole and come to their senses to see the error of their ways, both during and after undergoing the necessary steps as a consequence of their actions.

We ask this petition in Jesus' name. Amen.

Chapter 3

The Vision

A condensed version of this experience was shared in my published book, "The Question of Eternity," released in 2007 and again in 2015.

I am so often reminded that our lives—like vapors of smoke are transient and delicate, existing for a moment then disappearing. As beautifully stated in James 4:13-14 [13] *Go to now, ye that say, Today or tomorrow we will go into such a city, and continue there a year, and buy and sell, and get gain:* [14] *Whereas ye know not what shall be on the morrow. For what is your life? It is even a vapor, that appeareth for a little time, and then vanisheth away."*

We often fail to grasp the rapid pace of life's cycle and how swiftly we transition from celebrating the miracle of birth to mourning the loss of a loved one. Sometimes, all it takes is a single, life-altering event for us to confront our own vulnerability to realize just how delicate the thread of life truly is. This realization, while sobering, also underscores the importance of cherishing each moment, for our time here is but a brief sojourn in the grand tapestry of eternity.

Several years ago, I had a dream that served as a stark revelation of my vulnerability. In this dream, I was in the familiar surroundings of my parents' home in London, England. I was sitting alone on my bed in the comforting silence of the room.

Without any forewarning, an unexpected sensation began to ripple through me. I started to experience chest pains, each throb a jarring reminder of my mortality. The sudden onset of discomfort, piercing through the tranquility of the dream, emphasized the unpredictable nature of life and the fragility of our existence.

As I sat there, the pain intensified, each wave more overwhelming than the last. It was as if something had clamped around my chest, squeezing the very life out of me. My upper arm throbbed in unison with my racing heartbeat, the pain so severe that it felt like needles piercing through my skin. In my dream, I did not think of crying out for help, perhaps because the pain was so severe that I could not get the words out.

Although this experience is based on a dream, it was unfolding with an abundance of intricacies. For instance, the radiance of the London streetlights penetrated my window, their inexplicable visibility casting a comforting amber glow that stood in stark contrast to the chilling trepidation that gripped me. As I grappled with this suffering in solitude, time seemed suspended.

In the dream, I found myself walking into the doctor's office. After undergoing a series of tests, I sat in the hushed silence of the examination room. The air was thick with anticipation, and the sterile scent of sanitizers heightened my senses. I was waiting—waiting for words that would chart the course of my future.

The doctor finally entered; his face etched with a somber expression that spoke volumes even before he uttered a single word. His gaze held a gravity that seemed to weigh heavily in the room, casting a palpable tension even before the words could escape his lips.

His prognosis was delivered with a solemnity that immediately anchored my heart to despair. "There is nothing more we can do," he said, his voice steady yet tinged with a hint of regret. "Go home and get your business in order, for you are going to die." His final words hung in the air like a guillotine, poised to sever the thin thread of hope I had been clinging to.

I grappled with the stark reality of my impending death. The world around me continued at a relentless pace, oblivious to the storm raging within my soul. Yet, in this crucible of uncertainty, I discovered a profound truth that resonated with the core of my Christian faith. Quite suddenly and unexplainably, I felt no fear of death at all—instead, a profound peace enveloped my entire being.

In all its fragility, life is a tapestry woven with threads of joy, sorrow, love, and loss. Each moment is a precious gift, not to be squandered or taken for granted. The doctor's grim words, though they seemed like a sentence, became a clarion call to live with intention, to cherish every breath, and to leave a legacy of love and faith that would outlive my earthly body.

I was reminded of the scripture in Ecclesiastes, which captures the seasons of our lives and their divine purpose for every event:

1 *To every thing there is a season, and a time to every*
purpose under the heaven:
2 *A time to be born, and a time to die; a time to plant,*
and a time to pluck up that which is planted;
3 *A time to kill, and a time to heal; a time to break*
down, and a time to build up;
4 *A time to weep, and a time to laugh; a time to mourn,*
and a time to dance;
5 *A time to cast away stones, and a time to gather*
stones together; a time to embrace, and a time to refrain
from embracing;
6 *A time to get, and a time to lose; a time to keep, and a*
time to cast away;
7 *A time to rend, and a time to sew; a time to keep*
silence, and a time to speak;
8 *A time to love, and a time to hate; a time of war, and*
a time of peace.

— ECCLESIASTES 3:1-8

This passage reminds us that every moment in our lives has a purpose orchestrated by God's divine plan. It encourages us to trust in His timing and embrace each season with faith and understanding.

As I pondered how to share this devastating news with my loved ones, I decided to express it through a heartfelt letter. When my mother and daughter arrived home, I handed them the letter and stood at a distance as they absorbed the news. In the letter, I urged them not to mourn for me, assured them of my unwavering love, and expressed that all was well with my soul. I comforted them with the promise that we would reunite in heaven, where peace and joy would abound.

To my utter astonishment, they exhibited perfect peace upon reading it—no trace of sadness, only serenity and acceptance, as if they were fully prepared for the news.

As I began the solemn task of putting my affairs in order, I came to a profound realization: it was not the material possessions that held true value. Instead, it was the relationships I had nurtured and cherished over the years, the forgiveness I had both granted and sought and the peace I had made with my God. My impending death was not an end but rather a transition to a new beginning—a journey from the temporal earthly realm to the eternal, immortal realm. For in Christ, death is not a defeat but a victory—a triumphant transition from mortal life to eternal life. In the face of adversity, let us stand firm in our faith, for it is through Christ that we gain the strength to overcome.

To my fellow Christians, I share this heartfelt message: Let us live each day with passion and sincerity, embracing every moment as an opportunity to reflect the love of Christ in our words and actions. Let us strive to be vessels of His grace, radiating His love and compassion to all we encounter. We must remember that our time here on earth is but a prelude to the glory that awaits us in His heavenly kingdom.

A Divine Encounter: A Visit from an Angel

As the night deepened, the stillness of the house seemed to echo the tranquility in my heart. The rhythmic ticking of the clock on the mantle helped me reflect on the day's revelations and the profound peace that had settled within me. It was as if each tick of the clock was knitting my spirit closer to what awaited me.

The book resting upon my lap lay open as I penned

down my reflections, not just as a record of events but as a testament to the unwavering faith that had taken root in my being.

In that stillness, I pondered many things in my communion with the Lord. My concerns for my family, particularly their well-being in my absence. Yet, entrusting all my hopes and dreams at the feet of God Almighty, I felt profound peace and assurance. I knew they were cradled in the palm of His hands, and they would be cared for.

At around 2 a.m., my ponderings were abruptly interrupted. I became acutely aware of a presence in the room with me. Turning my head slowly, I was met with the most marvelous sight. There, standing in the middle of the room, to my astonishment, was an angel of the Lord!

As strange as it may sound, I felt neither alarm nor fear in his presence. I sat there on my bed, awestruck, as the angel stood silently, emanating a serene demeanor. I realized that he may have been standing there for quite some time, observing me, before I became aware of his presence. This divine encounter, this visit from an angel, was a moment of awe and total reverence.

Our eyes locked for a fleeting moment before he slowly bowed his head, his hands clasped together in a gesture of prayer. I watched, captivated, as this solemn tableau unfolded before me. Then, with grace, he gradually lifted his head and fixed his gaze upon me.

A deep connection resonated between us, a silent understanding that transcended the need for words. It was as though I knew him; he, in turn, knew everything about me. This connection was profound and inexplicable.

Words fall short of capturing the overwhelming sense of peace that washed over me, the profound warmth that radiated from his presence. A wave of curiosity, wonder, and excitement surged through my entire being, each emotion more intense than the last. It was as if a dam had burst within me, allowing these feelings to overflow and fill me with a sense of astonishment.

Despite the palpable strength of his power, there was an inherent gentleness about him. When he looked at me, his gaze held a depth of understanding that seemed to pierce through to the very core of my being. His eyes, which must have witnessed countless wonders since the dawn of his creation, were in that moment, focused solely on me.

I felt a profound connection as I sat in the awe-inspiring presence of God's holy angel. It was as if he could perceive my thoughts, delving into the deepest recesses of my being. Then, he communicated with me in a manner that transcended the need for spoken words. Without opening his mouth or uttering a single word, his message was conveyed—a clear word without moving his lips—words that were distinct and became instantly etched into my thoughts, reaching into the very essence of my being. Man's limited ability to comprehend the power of God is just that: limited. God is a Spirit; and they that worship Him must worship Him in spirit and in truth (refer to John 4:24).

As he continued to communicate, my understanding began to unfold, each revelation bringing clarity. The angel conveyed his divine mission, a directive from God Himself. His purpose was one of transition; he had been sent to escort me home.

The realization that I was to be escorted home by God's holy messenger filled me with an overwhelming sense of joy and honor. This was a testament to the boundless compassion of the living God, our Creator.

The angel's appearance bore a man's resemblance, yet something about him transcended human form. He radiated power and authority, unlike any mortal man. His demeanor was calm yet instilled with a seriousness that spoke volumes about his divine mission, and that was to fulfill the Will of Almighty God!

His presence reminded me of the solemnity and seriousness of the angel who appeared to Moses in the Book of Exodus. Like that divine messenger, he was a beacon of God's power and authority.

This story unfolds in the aftermath of the Children of Israel's liberation from over four centuries of bondage in Egypt—a monumental event led by Moses and his brother Aaron. The Lord God conveyed a profound message to Moses for His people. He assured Moses that He would send His Angel before them as a divine guide to lead them through the wilderness and into the place that He, the Lord, had prepared for them. This divine promise was a beacon of hope and assurance, reminding the Israelites of God's unwavering presence and guidance as they embarked on their journey to the Promised Land.

However, this divine guidance came with a solemn warning. The people were instructed to obey the voice of His Angel and not provoke him. This was not merely a suggestion but a divine mandate. The Angel was not to be taken lightly, ignored, or disobeyed, for he would not pardon their transgressions. This was because God's name, His divine presence, resided within the Angel.

> 20 *Behold, I send an Angel before thee, to keep thee in the way, and to bring thee into the place which I have prepared.*
>
> 21 *Beware of him, and obey his voice, provoke him not; for he will not pardon your transgressions: for my name is in him.*

[22] But if thou shalt indeed obey his voice, and do all that I speak; then I will be an enemy unto thine enemies, and an adversary unto thine adversaries.

[23] For mine angel shall go before thee, and bring thee in unto the Amorites, and the Hittites, and the Perizzites, and the Canaanites, the Hivites, and the Jebusites; and I will cut them off.

— EXODUS 23:20-23

In the presence of the angel, time lost its meaning. I could not discern whether seconds, minutes or even hours had passed, for time appeared to stand still in this divine encounter. I found myself looking at the angel, and without uttering a word or moving my lips, I heard my own voice within me. It was a request for additional time—a few more precious moments in this earthly realm to bid my loved ones farewell.

The thought that my request for more time might be denied did not perturb me. Instead, I found myself enveloped in a serene acceptance of whatever God's will might be for me. With this acceptance guiding me, I moved through the house, each step carrying the weight of unspoken farewells.

I entered the rooms where my loved ones lay in peaceful slumber, their breaths a soft symphony in the quiet night. I reached out, my arms wrapping around them in a tender embrace, a silent farewell that spoke volumes. As I held them close, silent thoughts and unspoken words lingered in my heart.

A fleeting thought crossed my mind, a vision of a future that might unfold without my presence. I reflected on my daughter, her life devoid of me when suddenly a pang of anxiety gripped my heart; the fear of my absence cast a shadow over the peacefulness of the moment.

But as quickly as the worry arose, it dissipated like mist. A profound sense of peace enveloped me with a divine assurance that surpassed all earthly concerns. In that very same moment, I promptly understood that the same loving God who created and fashioned the heavens and the earth and everything therein—the omnipresent God—would cradle my daughter's future. I stood reassured that she would never walk alone, for God's grace would be with her.

And so, with a heart fortified by faith and a spirit calmed by God's divine assurance, I went back to my room and stood in the presence of the angel, ready to face whatever was in store.

My escort stood patiently waiting. Again, our spirits communicated in a language beyond words that resonated within my being. Turning to him, I declared in my spirit that I was now ready!

I instinctively knew what to do. Walking slowly toward the angel, I wrapped both arms around him and closed my eyes. As I clung to the angel, I immediately felt that I was being carried to a huge open window or large opening. Without warning, the angel took a colossal leap and surged into the night atmosphere.

Flight by Night

We soared through the air at an incredible speed—faster than the speed of light! The Earth faded away, appearing as a distant memory. With my eyes closed, I could see the stars spread like a blanket across the vast expanse of the heavens.

I was acutely aware of my surroundings and knew what

was transpiring on Earth. I knew the date, time, and the unfolding events. Man's masquerades were unceasing! I could see them running back and forth, executing whatever evil their imaginations conceived. Wherever I focused my attention, I could see them clearly—as if I were standing beside them.

I observed humans on Earth with a mixture of curiosity and pity. They were oblivious to the events taking shape around them. I could see them, but they could not see me!

In one instance, I witnessed a group of soldiers in matching uniforms. Their commander, an aged man with stern features, displayed a mischievous grin, a cigar perched between his lips as he addressed them. They were ready for battle at a moment's notice! They did not realize that the conflicts of man were temporal and fleeting; everything would be left behind, and someone else would take their place. They did not know that life flees in a moment—in the twinkling of an eye!

I shifted my attention to another part of the world. Women in white gowns were smiling and laughing, full of excitement, for they were about to be wedded. In yet another area, I saw starving, orphaned children sitting naked on dirty roadsides with arms outstretched. They longed to be held, loved, and fed. Their unwashed bodies blended with the ashen and dusty ground, their arms outstretched, yearning for compassion. I felt a pang of sympathy for the suffering children whom passersby totally disregarded. Well-dressed people hurried past them, ignoring their cries. It struck me how self-centered and callous individuals can be. I wondered how these individuals would react if they knew I could see them. Worse still, how would they react if they realized that the Lord also sees them?

In various locations across California, I observed smoke rising from below the ground, reminiscent of the aftermath of an underground volcanic eruption. As I extended my gaze, I noticed this phenomenon occurring in other cities as well throughout the United States. In that moment, I felt the profound presence of the Lord Jesus beside me. In my spirit, I caught a glimpse of Him, and tears streamed down His cheeks as He turned to look at the areas where the smoke was emerging. There was an overwhelming sadness in His eyes. I struggled to comprehend the depth of His sorrow or the reason for the smoke.

By simply focusing my attention, I was able to see any nation and tongue immediately. I understood, undoubtedly, that God Almighty and His angels see all things on Earth and take note of them, for nothing is hidden from God.

The Angel ascended even higher into the heavens, revealing a profound truth: those who accept the Lord Jesus Christ into their hearts receive forgiveness of sins, are new creations in Christ Jesus, and are future citizens of heaven. They are being escorted home daily, but this divine transition goes unnoticed by the inhabitants of the earth. As Psalm 116:15 states, [15] *Precious in the sight of the Lord is the death of His saints.*

The god of this age, the devil, has blinded the minds of unbelievers. They do not see the glory of God or the hope of eternal life because they are preoccupied with worldly affairs and earthly pleasures. They fail to realize the shortness of time and their need for repentance. I feel deeply sad for those who have already left this world while lost in their sins. Unfortunately, it is too late for them.

In this vision, I had finished my race, fought the good fight, and kept the faith. Now, I was ready to receive the crown of life, the reward of the righteous as beautifully recorded in 2 Timothy 4:6-7: [6] *For I am now ready to be offered, and the time of my departure is at hand.* [7] *I have fought a good fight, I have finished my course, I have kept the faith:*

A sense of fulfillment and peace washed over me as I stood at the threshold of eternity, knowing that I had remained steadfast in my faith and devotion to the Lord.

The angel continued to soar even higher, and though my eyes remained closed, the heavens suddenly became illuminated. The light was so brilliant that I could perceive its radiance even with my eyes tightly shut. The presence of the Son of God permeated the atmosphere, rendering the sun unnecessary. We journeyed through the universe and galaxy to a brand-new heaven. Christ's presence not only provided light but also warmth in the atmosphere.

The tremendous brightness far surpassed that of the Earth's sun. It was unlike anything I had ever seen or experienced. The atmosphere was pure, unadulterated, and holy, filled with a gentle, soothing warmth that enveloped me. A profound sense of peace and serenity washed over my soul. The fragrance of the air was sweet and refreshing, like a blend of the most delicate flowers. My escort and I embarked upon a new heaven, far above Earth's heaven.

Suddenly, I became acutely aware that my body had transformed. It was akin to changing garments, a seamless and gentle transition. This transformation occurred as I soared through the air. I felt a tingling sensation spread throughout my body, as if every cell were being renewed and revitalized.

The pain in my chest had completely vanished, replaced by an overwhelming sense of peace and tranquility. My body felt lighter, almost weightless, and a warm, comforting energy enveloped me. The lyrics of an old hymnal that I had sung countless times at church arose within me:

Oh, I want to see Him, look upon His face,
There to sing forever of His saving grace;
On the streets of glory, let me lift my voice,
Cares all past, home, at last, ever to rejoice.

("Oh, I Want to See Him," Words and music by Rufus H. Cornelius, 1916).

Divine praise enveloped me, and anticipation settled upon my soul—I stood on the precipice of encountering His presence. A great feeling of expectancy overshadowed me as I prepared to embark upon His presence and meet my Maker. And then, without warning, I awoke!

My eyes flew open, and I sprang out of bed. It felt as though my spirit had abruptly reclaimed its earthly vessel. I stood at the bedside, trembling, my heart racing, and my mind reeling from the vivid experience.

Outside, the sun had risen, but the earth wore a vastly different visage—it looked dirty, dull, and gloomy. The once vibrant sun, which used to cast a golden glow, now seemed muted and lackluster. The flowers, once bursting with color and life, appeared wilted and lifeless. The lush greens of the trees and grass had faded to a suffocating, pale tone, and the air felt heavy and oppressive.

This stark transformation from the spiritual to the natural world left me pondering the fragility of our existence and the fleeting nature of earthly beauty. My thoughts turned to the people who are treading a different path, unacquainted with Jesus Christ. I wondered if they, too, felt the weight of this world and the emptiness that comes from being disconnected from Him.

It was a reminder of the importance of sharing the light and hope of Christ with others so that they, too, may experience the true beauty and peace that come from knowing Him.

Many people only want to amass wealth, fame, and accolades through any means possible, while lavishing themselves with treasures that rust and fade. They invest their time and energy in things that don't last, things that bring only momentary satisfaction. They serve other gods and believe that all roads and all religions lead to God in heaven. They scoff at those who truly serve the "One True God," dismissing faith as a relic for the feeble-minded, the desperate, and the fanatical.

These are the ones who are rich in this world, the wicked, the corrupt, and the prideful. They have built their empires upon quicksand, pursuing self-gratification, hedonistic pleasures, and egocentric ambitions. Their lives are a testament to the futility of chasing after worldly gains, for their foundations are unstable, and their pursuits are ultimately empty.

But oh, how they missed the power, the love, and the opportunity to know the "true and living God" because they rejected the invitation of salvation. In their blindness, they forfeited redemption and traded it for the pleasures of this life. May we all come to the knowledge of the truth before it is too late!

> [18] *And if the righteous scarcely be saved, where shall the ungodly and the sinner appear?*
>
> — 1 PETER 4:18

Chapter 4

The Encounter

I stood at the threshold of an open door, captivated by the scene unfolding before me. There, in all his majesty, stood a large Angel—a celestial being adorned in robes of the purest white. Beneath his mighty wings were hands that bore a striking resemblance to those of a human, a harmonious blend of the divine and the earthly.

Though he stood across the street, his presence was palpable, as if he were right beside me. Every detail of his angelic form was vividly etched in my mind.

Without uttering a single word, I communicated with him. My lips remained motionless as I posed the question, "How can I walk in the spirit realm? I want to experience it."

In response, he reached out, his hand making contact with my head. With deliberate intent, he pulled my spirit from within me, starting from my head. A sensation of wonder enveloped me as he freed my spirit from its physical, earthly shell.

Untethered and liberated, I queried the Angel, my voice

tinged with uncertainty, "How can I be certain that my spirit has truly departed from my body?"

The Angel's steady gaze shifted over my shoulder to what lay behind, and he proclaimed, "Your body is right there behind you."

I turned, and there it was—my physical form slumped over the dining room table, appearing as if in a deep slumber. The lines between death and sleep blurred, for in that moment, death and sleep seemed indistinguishable to me.

Stepping out of the house, I walked down the pathway to a white gate. Its picket fence encircled the front courtyard. I ventured through the open gate and followed the Angel as he guided me around a bend.

Together, we embarked on an ascent, climbing a gentle incline. As we ascended, my eyes were drawn to others approaching us, their figures draped in garments of the purest white. Upon reaching us, they joined our ascent, striding up the incline alongside us. Glancing down at my own attire, I realized that I, too, was adorned in a garment of the same radiant white. The eight of us moved in unison, a harmonious procession ascending the incline.

Ahead, three figures—two men and a woman—were engaged in a profound discussion, their conversation echoing the depth and wisdom of theologians, those esteemed scholars of the Word of God. Intriguingly, though their lips remained still, I could hear and comprehend their discourse.

Trailing behind us, two men continued their journey, deeply engrossed in their own conversation.

Between the angel and me stood a woman, as silent as I was. We exchanged no words yet there was an unspoken bond, a shared connection that we were on our journey to our heavenly abode.

A question lingered in my thoughts, and I turned to the Angel without opening my mouth and asked, "How can I discern that I am walking in the spirit realm? I don't feel any different."

To my surprise, all the conversations around me came to a halt as I addressed the angel with my question. My fellow travelers paused, then turned their heads and fixed their gaze upon me and the angel. They heard my question, which was addressed to the angel and captured in the spirit realm, audibly to all present.

Even after witnessing my own body slumped over the dining room table, I dared to seek further clarification. My audacity to question the angel fostered a collective curiosity that was etched on their faces.

The Angel embodied patience and remained silent. His eyes were steady, unwavering, and locked with mine. In that moment, he offered no verbal response despite my anticipation, I awaited his reply, but it never came, and a wave of self-disappointment surged within me for having posed the question. With that feeling still echoing in my consciousness, I abruptly awoke from sleep.

In the Book of Ezekiel Chapter 8, the prophet shares a profound vision, where he describes an encounter with an angel of the Lord who reached out his form of a hand and takes hold of him by the lock of his hair. In this vision, the Spirit elevates him between the earth and the heaven, positioning him in a realm beyond the physical.

I lay still on my bed, immersed in contemplation of this profound dream. Ezekiel 8:1-3 began to surface within my mind and compelled me to record my experience.

1 *And it came to pass in the sixth year, in the sixth month,*
in the fifth day of the month, as I sat in my house, and the
elders of Judah sat before me, that the hand of the Lord
God fell there upon me.

2 *Then I beheld, and lo a likeness as the appearance of*
fire: from the appearance of his loins even downward, fire;
and from his loins even upward, as the appearance of
brightness, as the color of amber.

3 *And he put forth the form of a hand, and took me by*
a lock of mine head; and the spirit lifted me up between the
earth and the heaven, and brought me in the visions of
God to Jerusalem, to the door of the inner gate that looketh
toward the north; where was the seat of the image of
jealousy, which provoketh to jealousy.

— EZEKIEL 8:1-3

Chapter 5

Stay in the Car

It was seven-thirty in the evening when I left my office and entered the underground parking lot. The frigid night air clung to my bones and the darkness made it feel more like midnight. I worried whether the chilly air would drain my car's battery, but to my surprise, the engine roared to life when it started.

As I navigated on the bustling expressway, my vehicle began to jolt in a distressing rhythm each time the traffic flow came to a sudden halt. A wave of worry washed over me, amplified by the stark realization that I was without the comfort of a phone.

The traffic was surging forward more fluidly in the middle lane; I swiftly maneuvered my vehicle into it, hoping to evade the jarring stops that were all too frequent and minimize the strain on my fluctuating engine while keeping pace with the relentless rhythm of the expressway.

As we embarked on an uphill incline, my vehicle began laboring against the ascent while the other vehicles rushed down the other side with momentum. The expressway was pulsing with a diverse array of vehicles, including sedans, SUVs, and eighteen-wheelers.

Suddenly, without warning, the engine stuttered and then fell ominously silent. I didn't surrender to panic; instead, instinct swiftly kicked in. I turned the key while pressing on the gas pedal once, twice, several times in succession, hoping to bring the engine back to life. But the only response was a clicking sound before it faded into silence, amplifying the gravity of the situation.

Then, the heavens opened, and the rain began to fall, starting as a gentle tapping on the roof but quickly escalated into a relentless downpour, cascading onto my windshield in an unyielding onslaught. They struck the glass with such force that it created a symphony of nature's fury. Blind spots surrounded me—I found myself besieged by unseen threats. My vehicle was devoid of its headlights, interior lights, and hazard lights; all had succumbed to the lifeless battery. Even the windshield wiper, my last line of defense against the elements, had ceased to function.

The middle lane had morphed into a perilous trap. The monstrous eighteen-wheelers loomed ominously in my rearview mirror, their brakes screeching in intensity as they were forced to decelerate to avoid crashing into my lifeless vehicle.

There I was, stranded in a vessel without light and life, a mere shadow against the relentless onslaught of the rain. The downpour was merciless, obliterating all visibility from my windshield and leaving me blind and vulnerable in the unforgiving night.

My mind was suddenly flooded with the vivid memory of an incident that had transpired just a week prior. It was a late-night drive, around eleven-thirty, on an eastbound highway bathed in the comforting glow of well-placed lighting.

I was driving steadily in the far-right lane when, in the rearview mirror, I noticed a menacing vehicle approaching mine. It was closing in at an alarming speed, its movements erratic and unpredictable. A shiver of fear ran down my spine as I envisioned the potential disaster of it colliding with my vehicle.

I indicated and maneuvered my vehicle into the relative safety of the middle lane. The driver, seemingly oblivious to the danger he posed, sped past me. He then darted in front of me, narrowly avoiding a collision. His reckless driving and disrespect for road rules and the safety of others and himself left an indelible mark in my memory.

I gently eased off the accelerator and stayed back as I watched the car ahead accelerate even further. Abruptly, the night was shattered by a horrifying sound as chaos erupted —twisted metal, human screams, and the screeches of tires skidding against the asphalt filled the air.

The speeding vehicle collided with a disabled car stranded in the middle lane, its hazard lights still blinking. A wave of shock surged through me as I maneuvered my car to the side of the road. The collision was inevitable; the aftermath, I feared, would be devastating.

Bystanders, their faces etched with dread, fumbled with their phones and dialed 9-1-1. The scene was a grim reminder of the fragility of life and the devastating consequences of reckless driving.

Without a moment's hesitation, I found myself instinctively sprinting toward the disabled vehicle, feeling compelled to help. As I neared, a chilling sight met my eyes —a baby car seat violently hurled from the back to the front during the collision, pressed hard against the windshield due to the brutal force of the impact.

The vehicle was eerily empty, but then a figure emerged from the shadows. A woman, her face ashen, her eyes wide and filled with disbelief, walked toward me. Only moments before, she had vacated her car, seeking refuge in the embankment.

Had she chosen to remain, or if her infant had been fastened in the car seat, the aftermath would have painted a drastically different picture. She confided in me later that her baby was safe at home. Had she not made the split-second decision to distance herself, she would have been catapulted through the windshield.

With a sense of urgency, I hastened toward the other vehicle, the one driven by the individual responsible for the accident. He was conscious, his body smeared with blood, and his hands desperately clinging to the steering wheel. His face was a canvas of agony, his broken nose bleeding profusely and staining his shirt.

Amid the chaos, I managed to ask him if he was alright, reassuring him that help was swiftly on its way. He didn't want me to leave his side. His body was trembling, a physical manifestation of the dread he felt for the potential consequences of his actions.

The woman, the victim of the vehicular accident, approached with fury swirling in her eyes and rebuked him strongly for his reckless conduct. Amidst the escalating tension, I gently reminded her that, despite the material damage, we should find consolation in the fact that lives were spared.

The memory of that incident, just a week prior, weighed heavily on my mind. My once-reliable car had broken down on a desolate stretch of the expressway, where the absence of overhead lights plunged the road into darkness. Visibility was severely limited, with only the headlights of passing vehicles piercing the gloom.

As I considered stepping out of the vehicle, I was acutely aware of the potentially fatal consequences of walking into the path of oncoming traffic. Yet, remaining inside the car, surrounded by metal and glass, left me feeling equally vulnerable. There was no safe option; each choice carried its own risks.

The relentless flow of traffic, each vehicle speeding past, heightened the sense of danger. I felt trapped, wondering how I would survive this ordeal. Outside, the rain was unrelenting, transforming the windshield into a blurred, watery canvas and further obscuring my view. The hope of rescue began to fade, and it seemed only a matter of time before an inevitable collision occurred.

With my eyes closed, I heard the screeching of brakes and the blaring of horns behind me, intensifying the urgency of the situation. In my desperation, I cried out to my Heavenly Father, my only hope. Despite my fears, I knew I was not alone.

In the profound recesses of my soul, I discerned the voice of the Holy Spirit articulating, *"STAY IN THE CAR, STAY IN THE CAR, AND YOU WILL NOT BE HURT."* These words, brimming with reassurance, instilled a sense of tranquility and solace in my distressed heart, albeit momentarily. Subsequently, the Spirit of the Lord stirred my memory, evoking the narrative inscribed in the Book of Acts, specifically Chapter 9 and Chapters 25 through 27.

Saul, who later came to be known as Paul (as referenced in Acts 13:9), was a Jew who cast a shadow of terror over the followers of Jesus Christ. He persecuted them with relentless fervor and was responsible for the martyrdom of His disciples. Their only crime was the steadfast proclamation of the Gospel of Jesus Christ, acknowledging Him as the risen Savior.

Embarking on a journey along the Damascus Road, Saul was armed with letters of authority from the high priest. These letters, addressed to the leaders of the synagogues, granted Saul the power to detain any individual who professed faith in Jesus Christ. Whether male or female, these believers were to be captured and forcibly brought to Jerusalem, where they would stand trial for their unwavering devotion to Jesus Christ.

Saul's unyielding drive to apprehend all believers was suddenly interrupted by a supernatural encounter from heaven. As he neared Damascus, a radiant light, brighter than anything he had ever witnessed, burst forth from the heavens. The divine brightness was so overpowering that Saul, overcome by the light and its intensity, was thrown off his horse and onto the ground. Amid this astonishing scene, a voice echoed from the heavens, resonating with profound authority, saying unto him, *"SAUL, SAUL, WHY PERSECUTE THOU ME?"* The voice, filled with a mix of stern admonition and gentle inquiry, left Saul in a state of awe and confusion, forever altering the course of his life.

Overwhelmed with fear, Saul, trembling, asked, "Who art thou, Lord?" And the response came, clear and resounding, *"I AM JESUS WHOM YOU ARE PERSECUTING, IT IS HARD TO KICK AGAINST THE PRICKS."* The men accompanying Saul were dumbfounded, having heard the voice echoing from the heavens, yet there was no physical presence to be seen. Their minds struggled to comprehend the magnitude of this divine intervention.

When Saul finally rose from the ground, he was met with a startling reality: he had been rendered blind. For three days, he grappled with the sudden loss of his sight.

Meanwhile, in Damascus, a man named Ananias, a devoted disciple of Jesus Christ, received a divine vision with instructions. The Lord commanded him to seek out Saul, lay hands on him, and pray for the restoration of his sight.

Upon receiving Ananias's prayer, Saul's sight was miraculously restored. But this was more than a physical healing; it marked the beginning of Saul's spiritual transformation. It was at this moment that Saul was entrusted with a monumental task—the Great Commission. He was chosen to spread the Gospel not just to the Gentiles and children of Israel but also to kings. This marked the start of Saul's journey as a tireless advocate for the faith.

Without a moment's delay, Saul began to proclaim the message of Jesus Christ in the synagogues, asserting with conviction that He is indeed the Son of God. However, his bold proclamation was met with hostility from the Jewish religious sects. They conspired against him, plotting to seize and execute him.

Undeterred by the looming threat, Paul continued to preach with unwavering courage and conviction, not just in Damascus but in numerous other cities as well. His audacious proclamation of faith eventually led to his capture. The very people he once stood with—the Jews and the religious sect—conspired against him, threatening to capture and slay him. Yet, Paul persisted in preaching boldly in Damascus and other cities before being finally captured and imprisoned by the Jews.

Now, bound by the shackles of captivity, he found himself aboard a ship charting its course toward the heart of the Roman Empire—Rome, Italy. His fate was to stand trial before a powerful ruler, Caesar Augustus, a consequence of his relentless preaching of Jesus Christ.

Nonetheless, on that treacherous winter voyage, a storm of severe intensity arose from the depths, its fury matched only by the turbulent winds that accompanied it. The ship was ill-equipped to withstand the tempest's onslaught.

The centurion, a figure of authority and the military commander responsible for the prisoners on board, along with the ship's owner, found themselves ensnared by a growing sense of dread that lives would be lost. The prisoners, too, were not immune to this fear.

Paul sensed the impending danger, foreseeing that the voyage would be perilous and that the ship would sustain considerable damage. For a brief respite, the wind, which had been blowing softly, suddenly transformed without warning into a tempestuous beast. For three relentless days, the storm's fury obscured the sun and the stars, plunging the ship into darkness.

Everyone on board—the crew, the prisoners, and the commanders—was gripped by fear and uncertainty. They struggled to maintain control as the ship was buffeted from all sides and began taking on water. The crew's efforts to keep the vessel afloat seemed increasingly futile. The sense of impending doom was palpable, hanging heavily in the air.

The relentless onslaught of the storm left no room for hope. The once gentle breeze had morphed into a ferocious tempest, its howling winds and crashing waves battering the ship mercilessly. The darkness was all-encompassing, creating an atmosphere of foreboding and despair.

As the storm raged on, the crew's desperation grew. Their attempts to navigate through the chaos were met with relentless resistance from the elements. The ship groaned under the strain, its timbers creaking and moaning as if in agony. The sense of impending doom was not just a feeling; it was a reality that loomed ever closer with each passing moment.

Yet, amid all these woes, Paul stood up and sought to encourage the men on the ship by sharing a vision he had experienced the night before. In this chaotic scene, Paul recounted how an angel of God had stood before him and declared, "Fear not, Paul, for there shall be no loss of any man's life among you, but only the ship." His words cut through the noise, bringing a glimmer of hope to the desperate crew. Paul continued, "Except these men abide (or remain) in the ship, you cannot be saved." The men listened intently, their eyes wide with a mixture of fear and hope as they clung to Paul's words like a lifeline. And so it was: no lives were lost, and all the occupants on board the ship were rescued.

As the rain unleashed its fury against the car windows, I clung to the divine message that had been imparted to Paul: "Stay in the ship, for there shall be no loss of lives."

Simultaneously, the gentle message from the Holy Spirit resonated within me: "Stay in the car, and you will not be hurt." These words, spoken with authority, were not merely advice and counsel; they were my lifeline and my comfort.

So, there I sat, isolated between metal and glass, my breath misting the windshield. Time blurred, and I wondered: "How long could one hold steady against the reality of the situation at hand and not feel some fear? How long until help finds me?" Suddenly, a loud tapping on the driver's side window, insistent and urgent, cut through the sound of the rain pounding on the car's frame. My gaze shifted to the driver's side window, where the relentless rain streaked the glass. There, obscured by the rivulets of water yet unmistakable, stood a silhouette.

His face remained a mystery, but it was his voice, the timbre of urgency—that pierced through the rain's loudness. "Put the car in neutral!" he yelled. I obeyed without hesitation, my hands moving swiftly to the gearshift and sliding it into that neutral space. The urgency in his voice left no room for doubt, and I felt a surge of adrenaline as I complied.

With unwavering determination, the mysterious figure pressed against the car's rear, his bare hands propelling it forward. The insensitivity of the impatient motorists reverberated as they honked in frustration. I wrestled with the steering wheel, guiding the vehicle onto the right embankment, two lanes over, narrowly avoiding disaster.

My rescuer remained a mystery, face concealed, yet his selfless act spoke volumes. He jeopardized his own safety to ensure mine. He was a silent hero in the chaos of that fateful moment.

Arriving on the narrow embankment, I felt the weight of my predicament. The driver's side was precariously suspended over the right lane of the expressway. My safety was threatened. I was still trapped and unable to exit the vehicle. I turned around, expecting to meet the man who had inexplicably propelled my vehicle with his bare hands to the embankment, but he was gone, nowhere to be found!

The nameless stranger, a special individual, had altered the course of my position. "Who was he? Where is he? Was he an angel sent to help me?" I pondered.

I cried out to the Lord, my voice a plea of desperation. "Lord," I prayed, "if I stay in the car, I will be hit."

And then, the Spirit of the Lord replied, *"STAY IN THE CAR, AND YOU WILL NOT BE HURT."*

I sat there, thankful for God's divine intervention again, but I knew I was still vulnerable. If I remained in that position, the oncoming traffic would catapult my car into chaos.

Before long, through the raindrops, I saw flashing lights approaching from behind. The driver, determined, struggled to stay close to the embankment, avoiding the traffic that roared past.

I sat there, not knowing what to do next. And then, another tapping on my driver's side window—urgent, insistent. "Put the car in neutral," the voice yelled through the closed window. "I will push you further into the embankment."

Without hesitation, I followed the instructions. The officer returned to his vehicle. Then, with metal against metal, he pushed my car using his own. Once safely on the embankment, he approached my vehicle and tapped on my window again. I opened the door, and there he stood—another rescuer, shielding me from the traffic as he led me to the safety of his cruiser. In that moment, I knew I was safe, having survived this ordeal.

The officer then guided me to the front door of the passenger side, his steps sure, his presence a calming force. Before pulling off, we sat and talked, with raindrops steadily tapping on the roof.

"How did you know where to find me?" I asked, my voice a whisper. "Dispatch received a call," he said, "from a man who told us a woman was stranded on the expressway; I was immediately dispatched."

As the car moved, we shared stories. I learned about his family, and he revealed his secret fear—that his line of work might one day rob his son of a father.

In the intimate exchange, I caught a glimpse of humanity concealed behind the uniform. As we departed the expressway, our destination was Dunkin' Donuts. There, amidst the aroma of coffee, I reached out to my loved ones. Seeking permission, I offered to pray for him and his family.

With heads bowed, I uttered words—a plea for God's divine intervention and protection in his life. Then I felt it: the Lord's presence enveloping us both. My new friend that evening accepted the Lord Jesus Christ into his heart.

As his patrol car's light receded into the night, racing toward another call, I couldn't suppress my gratitude to the Lord God for what He had done for me. I thanked Him for protecting me from certain death and for the encounter with the officer. I thanked Him for the stranger who stood behind my vehicle, pushing it with bare hands as the rain poured down unforgivingly upon him. Truly, the Lord is our refuge and strength:

> [1] *God is our refuge and strength, a very present help in trouble.*[2] *Therefore will not we fear, though the earth be removed, and though the mountains be carried into the midst of the sea;* [3] *Though the waters thereof roar and be troubled, though the mountains shake with the swelling thereof.*
>
> — PSALMS 46:1-3

Little did I anticipate that in the years to come, I would assume the role of a Sheriff chaplain, marking another significant chapter in my ministry. I journeyed alongside them, shared their rides, offered prayers for their well-being, and became a comforting presence as they unveiled fragments of their lives to me.

Beyond merely accompanying them, I held a position on the Executive Committee, conducting interviews with pastors who aspired to tread this path and serve as police chaplains. This role allowed me to contribute to the selection and guidance of those who would provide spiritual support to law enforcement personnel.

Throughout this journey, I gleaned a profound truth: God is omniscient, all-knowing. He possesses knowledge of every facet of our lives—past, present, and future. Even before we comprehend our own purpose, God has already charted our course and orchestrated our steps.

As I reflect on my experiences, I now understand that every moment, encounter, and challenge was part of a greater plan. God's wisdom and love have guided me, and I am grateful for the opportunity to serve and support those who dedicate their lives to protecting others.

Chapter 6

It Began Below Ground

It began as an unremarkable day, its routine unfolding predictably. My office overlooked the adjoining parking lot. Through the expansive window, I observed rows of parked cars, their surfaces glistening in the morning sun. The clock on my desk displayed 10:30 a.m., and as I sat there, my gaze shifted from the documents on my desk to the outside parking lot.

Nothing seemed out of the ordinary—until suddenly, in an instant, I was no longer confined by the physical boundaries of my office. Instead, I found myself suspended within the core of the Earth, captivated by my surroundings.

Miles beneath the Earth's surface, beyond the hard outer shell we tread upon, I beheld the image of a colossal hand within the Earth's inner core. It conveyed a sense of purpose and intention, and its sheer size symbolized power and authority.

The hand had four enormous fingers and an equally enormous thumb, with no adjoining wrist or forearm. It stood suspended in the void and darkness of the Earth's inner core. The fingers were separated and spread wide apart, and the hand remained suspended for its obscure purpose.

Observing further, I witnessed a sudden intrusion. A sharp object materialized, abruptly puncturing large holes in the thumb and each of the fingers with deliberate force.

Then, from the punctured fingers and thumb, large arteries began to grow out, pulsing with vitality and sprouting like vines. They grew until they became enormous, thick, and bulging. The arteries thrust through the Earth's core at tremendous speed, scattering in independent paths and diverging from the fingers, thumb, and hand. The arteries crisscrossed and zigzagged directly above and beneath each other, never detaching or dismembering. They remained connected to the hand, resembling a spaghetti junction of intertwined arteries.

From each artery, slender veins sprouted in substantial numbers. The veins mirrored the arteries, scurrying through the Earth's core with immense speed. They darted in self-directed directions, weaving intricate paths away from the hand, fingers, and arteries. They crisscrossed directly above and beneath each other, moving at excessive speeds through the Earth's core. Not once did the veins disconnect from the arteries.

The hand was fully alive, becoming a conduit for something malicious and evil. It expanded as though breathing, then contracted as though exhaling. Charged with an energy that defied natural laws, its breathing was both unexplainable and deeply unsettling. The breath—the inhale and exhale—was palpable, and the odor emanating from the hand was horrible. It drew from unseen reservoirs, and its fingers, arteries, and veins throbbed with a sinister rhythm that pulsed to life.

And then, without warning, the hand began to expel a liquid substance akin to contaminated blood. The veins and arteries responded, their walls pulsating as the tainted substance surged through them. They enlarged like balloons filled beyond capacity. The pressure mounted, threatening to rupture.

Instead of rupturing, they morphed into a malignant force of energy, their acceleration defying reason. With ferocity, they traveled through the core of the Earth, their velocity unmatched. I immediately sensed it—the vile substance that gushed through the hand, arteries, and veins was procreated and generated from the depths of Hell.

Intrusion and Devastation

Unpredictably, the arteries and veins altered their course and veered from their original path's trajectory. Instead, they synchronized in purpose and embarked upon a singular path. Their destination: the Earth's surface, the hard outer shell, the very ground upon which we walk.

The tips of the vessels transformed, no longer mere conduits of arteries and veins but becoming razor-sharp blades. Their purpose was clear: to breach the boundary of the Earth's crust and bring havoc upon the Earth.

As the arteries and veins ascended upward toward the Earth's surface, the crust, and the blades pierced through the Earth's crust with intensity and ferocity. The heart of the community, the churches, houses of worship, and synagogues—sanctuaries of faith—were not spared. The blades thrust themselves into their very foundations.

But the devastation did not end there. The malevolent

blades cut through the very foundations of businesses, disrupting the flow of commerce. Homes, once sanctuaries of warmth and safety, fell victim to the relentless intrusion. No place was immune; even the post office succumbed to the onslaught.

Law enforcement and government structures—emblems of order and authority—were not spared. The blades penetrated their cores, challenging the very bedrock of society. Every entity engaged in business, not just commerce but the essence of life itself, was targeted by the relentless assault.

To my utter horror, the hand unleashed its vile, contaminated blood-like substance through its fingers, arteries, and veins, infiltrating churches, houses of worship, and synagogues—those hallowed sanctuaries—rendering them infected. Every sacred place was tainted by this malevolent substance. The contamination spread further, seeping into post offices, law enforcement agencies, government structures, and every entity where business was conducted. Not a single building remained uncorrupted, untouched, unspoiled, or uncontaminated by the tainted, blood-like substance.

As I witnessed this, a profound sense of urgency gripped my heart. The Spirit of the Lord spoke to me, saying, *"THE ROOT OF CORRUPTION RUNS DEEP IN THIS COMMUNITY."* His words echoed in my mind, revealing the pervasive and insidious nature of the corruption that had infiltrated every aspect of society.

I was abruptly brought out of the vision, and at that moment, there was no interruption. This revelation had a profound impact on my actions. The clarity of the revelation left me in deep contemplation, and I was immensely grateful that the Spirit of the Lord graciously revealed this profound insight to me.

We often fail to comprehend that the malevolence manifesting on Earth originates from the depths of hell. Demons are being unleashed, utilizing human vessels to perpetrate the most diabolical acts. Regardless of the community, city, or nation, the same devil operates globally in a concerted effort to prevent humanity from surrendering to God Almighty. The enemy is a cunning and master strategist, relentlessly promoting evil with the goal of leading as many souls as possible to damnation alongside him.

Chapter 7

The Manhole

In yet another open vision, which occurred several months after the one mentioned in the previous chapter, I experienced a profound encounter. I had just arrived home after taking the afternoon off from work when I felt an overwhelming urge to go immediately before the Lord in prayer.

As I fell to my knees, I was suddenly caught up in an open vision. I found myself no longer in my living room but standing in an empty parking lot in a familiar area of town. From the parking lot, I observed a manhole in the middle of the roadbed with its cover on. A manhole provides an access point to pipes and underground tunnels in sewage drains and surface water drains.

As I stood there, the atmosphere felt eerily still, with an overcast sky casting a gray hue over the surroundings. The air was thick with an unsettling silence, broken only by the distant hum of traffic. The manhole cover, though seemingly ordinary, exuded an ominous presence. It was slightly rusted, with faint markings that hinted at years of wear and tear. The ground around it was cracked and uneven, as if the earth itself had been disturbed by something beneath.

Suddenly, the lid of the manhole began to move, shifting slowly upward from the inside. A low, grinding sound filled the air as the cover was raised further upward and then pushed to the side, revealing the dark abyss below.

Emerging from the manhole, feet first, was a figure clad in a white shirt with the sleeves torn off close to the shoulders. His white shorts reached just below his knees, revealing muscular and powerful legs. He was stout and powerfully built, with a large and strangely shaped head. His focus was fixed on the manhole, looking down into it.

As I watched, another figure emerged from the manhole, also feet first, but much smaller than the first figure. They were dressed identically, their movements synchronized as if they were part of a sinister dance. After both figures exited the manhole, neither of them turned their heads to look in my direction.

The first man resembled the Incredible Hulk, the fictional character created for Marvel Comics, which was aired in a television series. His muscular and bulky frame symbolized his immense strength and his destructive behavior when under stress.

Both figures turned their heads in one direction and walked side by side. It was then that I realized I was looking at demonic spirits from the pits of hell.

As they turned the corner and began walking down the bustling street, teeming with restaurants, large groups of people, night lifers, partygoers, loud band music, and scantily dressed individuals, the Spirit of the Lord spoke to me, saying, *"THERE ARE DEMONS WALKING AMONGST YOU, BUT UNNOTICED TO THE CHURCH."*

The manhole was situated in the same community where I had previously witnessed the dark hand, buried deep within the earth's core, spewing out a tainted, blood-like substance that infiltrated every facet of society where business was being conducted.

Chapter 8

Thus, My Heart was Grieved

For many weeks, my heart was deeply grieved as I observed the rampant wickedness perpetrated by the wicked. Despite their malevolent endeavors, they continue to prosper, deriving joy and financial gain at the expense of the gullible and naïve.

I have witnessed their flagrant abuse of power, their web of brazen lies and deception spun with impunity. They flaunt their misdeeds, moving unchallenged and unchecked. Meanwhile, the world groans under immense stress, with countless souls suffering and under pressure. Yet, the wicked, expecting unwavering support for their reprehensible undertakings, continue to thrive, seemingly untouched and uncaring by the hardships that plague others.

The disparity between the prosperity of the wicked and the suffering of others is a bleak reminder of the pervasive influence of evil in our world. It underscores the urgent need for justice and the importance of remaining steadfast in our commitment to truth and righteousness, even in the face of overwhelming adversity. This sentiment is echoed in Proverbs 14, which highlights the contrast between the wise and the foolish, the righteous and the wicked, and the ultimate consequence of their actions.

Asaph's Struggle with the Prosperity of the Wicked

In Psalm 73, Asaph begins by affirming, [1]*Truly God is good to Israel, even to such as are of a clean heart"* (v.1). However, by verse two, he confesses his near backsliding, [2] *But as for me, my feet were almost gone; my steps had well-nigh slipped* (v.2).

Asaph's despondency and discouragement stemmed from observing the prosperity and lavish lifestyles of the wicked. He struggled deeply with the apparent injustice of the wicked thriving while he, a righteous man, faced constant suffering and life's harshness. In this Psalm, Asaph admits his envy and pain; he was discouraged because the wicked enjoyed:

- Prosperity: Despite their wickedness, they lived in abundance.
- Ease: Their lives seemed free from the struggles and suffering he endured.
- Success: They thrived while he faced continuous hardship.
- The wicked seemed to possess an abundance of wealth and material comforts far beyond their needs or desires. Their wealth continued to grow, further entrenching their position of power and influence.
- They were corrupt; their actions were marked by

dishonesty and moral decay, yet they faced no immediate consequences for their actions.

- They were arrogant and full of pride; their success bred a sense of superiority and self-importance, leading them to look down on others.
- They did not experience trouble as other men. Unlike the righteous, the wicked appeared to live carefree lives, untouched by the common struggles and hardships of life.
- They were full of violence; their power and influence were often maintained through aggression and oppression.
- They were full of pride and arrogance and set their mouths against heaven in blasphemy against God, openly mocking and defying God, showing no reverence or fear of divine judgment.

Seeking Justice and Revelation

The wicked, with their evil thoughts, questioned God's knowledge and authority when they said, *[11] How doth God know? And is there knowledge in the Most High?" (v. 11).*

Asaph's internal conflict and envy of the nefarious prospering in their wickedness for gain highlights the profound struggle of maintaining faith and righteousness in the face of overwhelming adversity and moral corruption.

Questioning the Advantages of Serving God

Observing the stark disparities between the righteous and the unrighteous, he began to question the true advantage of serving the Lord God. In moments of doubt, he compared himself to others, failing to recognize God's provisions, protections, and blessings in his life despite his personal struggles.

However, his perspective underwent a profound transformation after he entered the sanctuary of the Lord. It was there, in the presence of the Divine, that he gained clarity and understanding. He realized that the prosperity of the wicked is fleeting, and their ultimate fate is one of destruction and eternal separation from God.

This revelation brought about a significant shift in his attitude. He came to understand that true prosperity is not measured by earthly wealth or success but by one's relationship with God and the eternal blessings that come from living a life of righteousness and faith. Asaph's sanctuary experience helped illuminate the fact that success for the wicked is only temporary, it also reaffirmed the enduring value of spiritual devotion and integrity.

Asaph then wrote:

> [21] *Thus my heart was grieved, and I was pricked in my reins.*
> [22] *So foolish was I, and ignorant: I was as a beast before thee.*
> [23] *Nevertheless I am continually with thee: thou hast holden me by my right hand.* [24] *Thou shalt guide me with thy counsel, and afterward receive me to glory.* [25] *Whom have I in heaven but thee? and there is none upon earth that I desire beside thee.* [26] *My flesh and my heart faileth: but God is the strength of my heart, and my portion for ever."*
>
> — PSALM 73: 21-26 KJV (KING JAMES VERSION

> [21] *When I saw this, what turmoil filled my heart!* [22] *I saw myself so stupid and so ignorant; I must seem like an*

animal to you, O God. [23] *But even so, you love me! You are holding my right hand!* [24] *You will keep on guiding me all my life with your wisdom and counsel, and afterwards receive me into the glories of heaven!*[b] [25] *Whom have I in heaven but you? And I desire no one on earth as much as you!* [26] *My health fails; my spirits droop, yet God remains! He is the strength of my heart; he is mine forever!*

— PSALM 73: 21-26 TLB (THE LIVING BIBLE)

Asaph now comprehended the fate awaiting those who rejected God when he wrote:

[27] *For, lo, they that are far from thee shall perish: thou hast destroyed all them that go a whoring from thee.* [28] *But it is good for me to draw near to God: I have put my trust in the Lord God, that I may declare all thy works.*

— PSALM 73: 27-28 (KJV).

Asaph's transformation in Psalm 73 is a profound journey from confusion and frustration to understanding and faith.

The Consequences of Rejecting God

When individuals and nations choose to embrace evil and reject God, turning their affections to false deities, they inevitably face consequences. This is not merely a form of punishment; it is the natural outcome of straying from the path of God's will and His laws.

Before God brings judgment upon a nation or people, He searches the hearts of men, knowing what is within.

"The heart is deceitful above all things, and desperately wicked: who can know it? I the LORD search the heart, I try the reins, even to give every man according to his ways, and according to the fruit of his doings."

— JEREMIAH 17:9-10

Proverbs 14:33-34 reminds us:

33 Wisdom rests in the heart of him who has understanding, but what is in the heart of fools is made known.34 Righteousness exalts a nation, but sin is a reproach to any people."

EXAMPLES OF GOD'S WARNINGS

Instructions Conveyed to Ezekiel to Warn the People (Ezekiel Chapters 2 & 3; Psalm 106):

Ezekiel, both a prophet and priest of ancient Israel, was commissioned by God to rebuke the Children of Israel for their many sins and rebellion against Him. The purpose was to lead them to repentance and avert further judgment.

The Children of Israel were in captivity, having been taken from Judah and exiled to Babylon. Ezekiel, though a righteous man, was also among the captives. The good suffered with the bad due to Israel's rebellion.

The objective of his warning was to bring the ungodly to repentance, encourage the righteous to avoid sin, and reveal the reasons for their suffering. The Jewish people had adopted the evil attributes of other nations, and in a vision,

God revealed to Ezekiel the wickedness the leaders were committing in secret. God's presence was no longer in the temple.

They worshipped the Sun in the temple; women wept and worshipped false deities; immoral sexual activities took place in the temple; they worshipped various images and unclean beasts, and they sacrificed their children to Baal.

Ezekiel was instructed to speak to the House of Israel and warn them to repent of their wrongdoings so they could be restored. Ezekiel was told not to be afraid but to speak the words that God had given him, whether they would listen or not. The Lord also told Ezekiel that he was made to be a watchman unto the House of Israel.

Warning to the Wicked

> 17 *Son of man, I have made thee a watchman unto the house of Israel: therefore, hear the word at my mouth, and give them warning from me.*
>
> 18 *When I say unto the wicked, Thou shalt surely die; and thou givest him not warning, nor speakest to warn the wicked from his wicked way, to save his life; the same wicked man shall die in his iniquity; but his blood will I require at thine hand.*
>
> 19 *Yet if thou warn the wicked, and he turn not from his wickedness, nor from his wicked way, he shall die in his iniquity; but thou hast delivered thy soul.*
>
> — EZEKIEL 3:17-19

Warning to the Righteous Man

[20] Again, When a righteous man doth turn from his righteousness, and commit iniquity, and I lay a stumbling-block before him, he shall die: because thou hast not given him warning, he shall die in his sin, and his righteousness which he hath done shall not be remembered; but his blood will I require at thine hand.

[21] Nevertheless if thou warn the righteous man, that the righteous sin not, and he doth not sin, he shall surely live, because he is warned; also thou hast delivered thy soul.

— EZEKIEL 3:20-21

Warnings to a Leader

During the reign of King Solomon, Israel's third King, who was the son of David, Israel's second King; he received warnings as he began to rebel against God. Solomon's disobedience led the children of Israel into idolatry and the worship of false deities. The nation, once devoted to the worship of the One True God and blessed with His formidable power, strength, and protection, strayed from God and became ensnared in the web of false worship. This turning away from the Lord their God is highlighted in the Book of Kings:

[1] But King Solomon loved many strange women, together with the daughter of Pharaoh, women of the Moabites, Ammonites, Edomites, Zidonians, and Hittites.

[2] Of the nations concerning which the Lord said unto the children of Israel, Ye shall not go in to them, neither

shall they come in unto you: for surely they will turn away your heart after their gods: Solomon clave unto these in love.

[3] And he had seven hundred wives, princesses, and three hundred concubines; and his wives turned away his heart.

[4] For it came to pass, when Solomon was old, that his wives turned away his heart after other gods: and his heart was not perfect with the Lord his God, as was the heart of David his father.

[5] For Solomon went after Ashtoreth, the goddess of the Zidonians, and after Milcom, the abomination of the Ammonites.

[6] And Solomon did evil in the sight of the Lord, and went not fully after the Lord, as did David his father.

[7] Then did Solomon build a high place for Chemosh, the abomination of Moab, in the hill that is before Jerusalem, and for Molech, the abomination of the children of Ammon.

[8] And likewise did he for all his strange wives, which burnt incense and sacrificed unto their gods.

— 1 Kings 11:1-8

God's Anger Revealed against Solomon

[9] And the Lord was angry with Solomon, because his heart was turned from the Lord God of Israel, which had appeared unto him twice,

[10] And had commanded him concerning this thing, that he should not go after other gods: but he kept not that which the Lord commanded.

[11] Wherefore the Lord said unto Solomon, Forasmuch

as this is done of thee, and thou hast not kept my covenant and my statutes, which I have commanded thee, I will surely rend the kingdom from thee, and will give it to thy servant.

— 1 KINGS 11:9-11

Solomon's transgression was particularly grievous due to his participation in the idolatrous practices of his wives, which included the abhorrent act of sacrificing human beings as worship to false gods. Each of his wives adhered to the worship of different deities, and Solomon, in his misguided devotion, offered sacrifices to each of their gods.

It is important to emphasize that Solomon had seven hundred wives, and three hundred concubines, as recorded in 1 Kings 11:3. These numerous alliances led Solomon's heart away from God, causing his downfall and the decline of Israel.

The command to refrain from marrying foreign women was not intended as a punitive measure but rather to ensure that the people remained faithful to the Lord God and served Him exclusively. However, Solomon defied this command and began to worship pagan deities such as Ashtoreth, Milcom, Chemosh, Molech, and Baal. Consequently, God raised up adversaries against Israel to execute His judgment upon them for their disobedience.

These verses underscore the profound truth that righteousness leads to the exaltation and honor of a nation, while foolishness and sin result in disgrace and downfall. When a society aligns itself with God's wisdom and righteousness, it flourishes and experiences His grace, mercy, and divine protection. Conversely, when it deviates from these divine principles, it inevitably suffers the natural repercussions of its actions.

> [34] *Righteousness exalteth a nation: but sin is a reproach to any people.*
>
> — PROVERBS 14:34

My Open Vision, A Storm Is Coming

It is imperative that we heed the lessons of history, as past generations have experienced the consequences of rebellion against God through the enactment of specific laws that goes against the principles of God. The same transgressions committed by the children of Israel and other nations in ancient times are being replicated today, both in secret and openly.

A few years ago, while I was a passenger in my daughter's vehicle, I experienced an open vision. Seated in the front passenger seat, my gaze wandered beyond the window and was drawn inexorably upward. My eyes drank in the boundless expanse of the azure sky, splendidly adorned with an array of white, fluffy clouds that created a perfect masterpiece.

The cloud formations meandered intermittently, guided gently by summer's mild breeze. As I marveled at the grandeur of God's magnificent creation, my train of thought were abruptly interrupted. The Holy Spirit spoke, His voice resonating profoundly within the innermost chambers of my being: *"ALTHOUGH THE SKY APPEARS CLEAR AND CALM NOW,"* He declared, *"A STORM IS COMING."* I paid heed to His words with unwavering attention.

"THIS IMPENDING STORM IS NOT ONLY A PHYSICAL MANIFESTATION OF RAIN, WIND, AND HAIL —IT WILL SIGNIFY A PERIOD OF GREAT TROUBLE. A STORM OF SORROW, SADNESS, AND FEAR. IT WILL BE A TIME WHEN THE FAITH OF MANY WILL GROW COLD, THEIR HEARTS SHALL FAIL THEM, AND THEY SHALL TURN AWAY FROM ME."

Immediately after these words, I saw myself with my children, suddenly suspended between the earth and the sky. My arms encircled them as we stood suspended in a desperate embrace, shielding against the inevitable troubles about to be unleashed upon Earth.

Without warning, we were assailed by gale-force winds, freezing rain, and large hailstones. Each strike threatened to dislodge me from my already unstable hold. The tempest raged with unparalleled fury, battering me repeatedly with such force that I was on the verge of losing my grip. As I fought with every ounce of strength, a wave of desperation and dread surged within me, fearing for the safety of my children and myself.

In that suspended moment, my faith was profoundly challenged. The storm's impact was not only tangible but also deeply spiritual. The winds battered not only the physical world but also the very core of my being. Fear and doubt gnawed at my resolve, threatening to tear us apart.

The fragility of our bodies, suspended in the face of danger, and our primal need for safeguarding were palpable. We held tightly onto each other, united against the merciless and unyielding storm. I clung on, not solely for my survival, but for the irreplaceable lives entrusted to my care. Amidst this chaos, there was a profound sense of God's presence. I felt the holy angels surrounding us, their protection a shield about us.

As the tempest raged and the winds bellowed their fury, I cried out to my Heavenly Father in a desperate plea. My cry for His intervention soared high above the tumultuous tempest, reaching an altitude that dwarfed the storm's wrath. The Lord heard my cry; He heard me! His divine presence was evident, though invisible to the eye. His omnipresence was our fortress, a defense against the tempest's wrath.

God's comfort arrived in my hour of need, infusing me with renewed vigor and unyielding resolve. His divine intervention rejuvenated my spirit. I found solace in the knowledge that we were not alone. The strength and courage that surged within me, fortifying me, were not of my own making but descended from the heavens, from God, who empowered me to withstand the storm.

Despite this invigoration, I was not totally shielded from the relentless terror wreaking havoc across our world. Though protected, I, too, had to face the storm. Even in my state of renewed strength, I found myself amid the chaos, confirming the indiscriminate nature of the catastrophe unfolding around us and that no one was exempt from it.

Around me, the scene unfolded: I witnessed the young and old, small and great, all overwhelmed by the tempest's fury. They clung desperately to anything—branches, railings, each other—as the wind howled and hail pummeled. However, the relentless and unforgiving force ripped control from their grasp. With arms flung wide open, they and their loved ones were swept away, lost in the turbulence and frenzy.

In the aftermath of this vision, my heart wept silently as I glimpsed a procession of students—youthful, carefree, and full of life and laughter—strolling along as our vehicle drove by them.

I understood they were unaware of the impending danger looming ahead; they couldn't see or know. They could not perceive the dark storm of terror and unrest that was approaching. The unsuspecting people remained blissfully ignorant. As we drove on, I carried the memory of their laughter with me, a heartrending reminder of their unawareness.

This experience serves as a reflective reminder of the enduring strength derived from faith and unwavering protection of our God. It also underscores the severe consequences that befall a nation and its people when they reject God. As the storm gathers and darkness looms, many will continue to choose the path of darkness, including believers who are not immune to temptation.

The allure and pressure to conform to worldly pleasures, materialism, quick riches, fame, and fortune are ever-present. Believers must also be vigilant not to fall prey to those who teach contrary to the Word of God, for many have been led astray and have fallen from grace.

As believers, we are the heralds of divine warnings, blowing the trumpet to all the world, sounding the alarm with a message of urgency. God is stirring our hearts, awakening us to our duty to warn people everywhere of the impending troubles on the horizon. Our mission is to guide them back to the path of righteousness, back to the loving embrace of God, our Father.

The Road to Redemption

In 2 Chronicles, Chapter 7, we witness a pivotal event in Israel's history before King Solomon had gone astray from the Lord. After completing the construction of the House of the Lord and his own house, Solomon experienced a divine visit. The Lord God appeared to him by night, delivering a solemn warning and a path to redemption.

The Lord declared that if He (the Lord) were to shut up the heavens so that there is no rain and command locusts to devour the land or send pestilence among His people as a result of their backslidings and sin, the Lord had prepared a way for the children of Israel to be restored back to Him. The Lord proclaimed:

> [12] *And the Lord appeared to Solomon by night, and said unto him, I have heard thy prayer, and have chosen this place to myself for an house of sacrifice.*
>
> [13] *If I shut up heaven that there be no rain, or if I command the locusts to devour the land, or if I send pestilence among my people;*
>
> [14] *If my people, which are called by my name, shall humble themselves, and pray, and seek my face, and turn from their wicked ways; then will I hear from heaven, and will forgive their sin, and will heal their land.*
>
> [15] *Now mine eyes shall be open, and mine ears attent unto the prayer that is made in this place.*
>
> — 2 Chronicles 7:12-15

This passage accentuates the importance of humility, prayer, and seeking God's face. When we approach God with a contrite heart, He promises to hear our prayers, forgive our sins, and bring healing to our land. However, this promise is accompanied by a stern warning.

> [19] *But if ye turn away, and forsake my statutes and my commandments, which I have set before you, and shall go and serve other gods, and worship them;*

[20] Then will I pluck them up by the roots out of my land which I have given them; and this house, which I have sanctified for my name, will I cast out of my sight, and will make it to be a proverb and a byword among all nations.

[21] And this house, which is high, shall be an astonishment to every one that passeth by it; so that he shall say, Why hath the Lord done thus unto this land, and unto this house?

[22] And it shall be answered, Because they forsook the Lord God of their fathers, which brought them forth out of the land of Egypt, and laid hold on other gods, and worshipped them, and served them: therefore hath he brought all this evil upon them.

— 2 CHRONICLES 7:19-22

As we reflect on these verses, let us strive to seek God's face earnestly, turn from our wicked ways, and remain steadfast in our faith, knowing that He is ever attentive to our prayers and ready to bring healing and redemption.

Chapter 9

Natural Progression - The Conveyor Belt of Life

One afternoon, while sitting alone by the ocean in my vehicle, I experienced an open vision. In this vision, I observed a colossal conveyor belt of life moving with hurried momentum. It was a remarkable sight as I witnessed thousands upon thousands of individuals—each a passenger on this relentless conveyor belt, journeying through existence. The conveyor belt symbolized the fast-paced nature of modern life, where individuals are swept along by the currents of daily existence without much control over their direction.

They sat on the conveyor belt without seats, in a state of complacency and comfortable relaxation, accepting their circumstances and riding the ceaseless belt of life passively, without questioning their path. Each person was unique, with expressions as diverse as they were, each face telling a different story. Yet, they were all part of the same collective journey. The conveyor belt moved them forward indiscriminately, propelled by an unseen force toward an unknown destination.

Amidst the continuous motion, I caught sight of a woman in a flowered summer dress, her legs outstretched on the conveyor belt, her back turned to the front. Her focused gaze rested upon the toddler sitting in front of her. A jar of baby food, its lid cast aside, served as nourishment for the child. With gentle care, she spooned sustenance into the child's mouth. She appeared serene and untroubled, seemingly unaware of the relentless belt moving rapidly toward an unknown destination. The world scrolled by, yet her attention remained steadfastly anchored to that small child.

A Quiet Rebellion

Around them, a scene unfolded—the thousands of fellow travelers, their expressions like weathered stones, bore silent witness. Unconcern and carefree were etched into their features, while tolerance shaped their emotions. They rode this conveyor belt of existence to an unknown, unspecified destination, each traveler carrying their own stories and burdens. As the conveyor rolled on, I wondered, "Did they know? Did they have a sense as to where the conveyor belt might be taking them?"

Amidst the ceaseless rhythm, my gaze rested upon a man—a silent figure who was in his late thirties or early forties. His attire spoke of dignity and purpose—a dark suit tailored to perfection. Seated upon the conveyor belt, he clung to his leather briefcase. Like all the others, he rode this relentless current, a passenger of fate. Yet, unlike the rest, he harbored a quiet rebellion—an urge to defy the norm and rise above the mundane.

I watched as he struggled against the relentless current of the moving belt, attempting to rise to his feet numerous times. His determination was calculated but ineffective. Even when he managed to stand, the unyielding and uncompromising conveyor belt swept him forward until he fell flat on his face, its pace unrelenting. Despite his repeated efforts to rise, his attempts were unsuccessful. So, there he sat on the conveyor belt, his legs dangling off the side, traveling in silent discontent.

A look of desperation and senselessness dashed across his face. He twisted his head, scanning the horizon. Left, then right, a swing of hope and another of despair. The conveyor belt carried him toward the unknown, indifferent to his silent plea. Engraved upon his face was a picture of bewilderment and frustration. His futile attempts to alter the course, to change the inevitable path, were met with insignificance and meaninglessness.

Nobody cared; their eyes were wide open, but their understanding was dull and void. Nobody spoke up, nobody communicated with each other, nobody offered help, and nobody questioned or assisted, even after his failed attempts to rise to his feet. They were veiled by the weight of their own journey. They were passengers without inquiry, swept toward an unknown horizon. Though they had eyes, they could not see, and though they had ears, they could not hear.

Something had happened to the world and its citizens; they appeared completely mindless and more robotic, except for the one man who attempted to change the trajectory of his life—to seek his freedom from the conveyor belt.

[5] They have mouths, but they speak not: eyes have they, but they see not.

— PSALM 115:5

[21] Hear now this, O foolish people, and without understanding; which have eyes, and see not; which have ears, and hear not.

— JEREMIAH 5:21

The thought reverberated in my mind: why did nobody glance his way? The man's struggle played out in silence; his attempts to alter fate were met with indifference. The conveyor belt, relentless and impartial, carried them all. Nobody responded. The unseen force driving this machinery did not heed their pleas. It knew no mercy, no pause. There was a quiet resignation among them. Nobody asked why, the purpose, the direction. Nobody wondered, queried, or questioned why they were where they were; they simply kept their silence with acceptance. The unseen force driving this machinery did not care for him or his defiance.

A stark bewilderment and frustration marked his face as he realized that his attempts to change or alter the course and direction of the conveyor belt, or his life, were futile and ineffective. In that suspended moment, the man, a mere speck, wrestled with forces beyond his control and comprehension. His briefcase was the only thing he clung to, his sole possession aside from the clothes on his back. And so, he remained; his face mirrored the collective plight of humankind. The conveyor belt carried him and them onward, its rhythm unbroken. His face was etched in stark realization that this was a place beyond choice or dissent. The unseen force that propelled them cared not for their desires or protests.

This open vision was both startling and unsettling. It led me to ponder. The scene was a stark contrast between passive acceptance and a solitary act of defiance. The man, with his briefcase held tightly, symbolized a rare determination to resist what was being forced upon him, while the others seemed resigned to their fate, devoid of any attempt to alter their course.

His opposition raised profound questions about human nature and the instinct for self-preservation. Why did all the travelers remain passive, their expressions blank and unresponsive, as they were carried along by the relentless conveyor belt? Was it a lack of awareness, a sense of helplessness, or a deeper resignation to forces beyond their control?

The man's struggles, though ultimately futile, highlighted individuality amidst the sea of conformity. His actions spoke volumes about the human spirit's capacity to strive and push against overwhelming odds. In contrast, the collective inaction of all the others underscored a troubling acceptance of their circumstances, a surrender to the unknown without question or resistance.

External Influences on Life Choices

Have you ever found yourself contemplating the profound influence that media, politicians, leaders, musicians, and fashion designers wield over our thoughts and actions? The media, with its pervasive reach, possesses the power to shape our perspectives. The narratives they craft can significantly sway our viewpoints, core values, and even govern our emotional responses. We often consume this information without the necessary critical analysis, a thought-provoking realization of how external influences can subtly control our private worlds.

Politicians, through their eloquent speeches, have the power to evoke emotions of hope, fear, or anger within us. We find ourselves clinging to their every word, fostering a sense of anticipation and belief in the prospect of positive transformation.

Fashion designers, with their creative prowess, dictate the trends, colors, and designs that dominate the fashion landscape. Regardless of how outrageous or unappealing these trends may be, we often conform, driven by a desire for social acceptance.

We are bombarded with advertisements and marketing strategies designed to create a sense of need and urgency. This culture encourages us to equate material possessions with happiness and success, often leading to a never-ending pursuit of the next best thing.

Fragrances, whether perfumes or colognes, possess a unique ability to captivate us. Their enticing aromas can sweep us off our feet, tapping into our emotional core. We often find ourselves willing to pay any price dictated by these scent creators.

Inked identity, or tattoos, is another powerful influence. Celebrities flaunt their ink designs, and suddenly, we yearn for a similar mark. Before we know it, we have joined the ranks of the "branded or labeled" individuals, becoming part of a larger collective identity.

All these factors contribute to us becoming walking billboards, our choices heavily influenced by external factors. It's a fascinating reflection of how our "individuality" is targeted, shaped, and molded by societal influences.

The Importance of Individuality

Observing the individuals on the conveyor belt, it appeared that no one possessed their own unique thoughts or individuality. If they did, they were disinclined to be nonconforming or "different" from the crowd. They allowed the thoughts, preferences, and aversions of others to become their own, willingly following the masses. We often find ourselves accepting anything and everything that is presented to us without any questions or challenges, consuming whatever is laid before us as truth, even if we suspect it to be deceitful and fallacious.

Consider the man on the conveyor belt, a symbol of independent thinking. He was able to discern that something was amiss. Regrettably, it was too late for him and all the others. His realization and subsequent actions, although commendable, were not timely enough to alter the inevitable outcome. He realized that the conveyor belt symbolized a lack of control over the management, governance, direction, and destiny in his life.

This revelation reveals the importance of reasoning and contemplation, expressing one's individuality in a world heavily influenced by external factors and demonic forces. It also emphasizes the necessity of taking deliberate steps to reclaim one's autonomy and align one's path with God's divine will for our lives, rather than being passively carried along by the currents of external pressures, and in this case, the conveyor belt of life.

Chapter 10

Do Not Be Deceived

In this vivid dream, my mother and I were shopping at a lively open-air market. Street vendors and merchants lined the narrow street for several blocks, adorning their stalls with vibrant and bountiful products. The market pulsed with life, businesses vivacious and full of charm, beckoning invitingly to passersby. Street merchants lined the cobblestone streets, their stalls a treasure trove of earth's bounties. Their wares were a feast for the senses—fruits that promised a burst of sweetness with each bite, vegetables still crisp with the morning dew, and an array of delectable delights that tempted even the most disciplined passersby.

Cradled in my forearm was a large straw basket, a nest for the carefully chosen fruits that I had selected. Together, my mother and I, a duo of discerning shoppers, navigated our way from vendor to vendor, stall to stall. We examined the fruits with a gentle touch, appreciating their vibrant colors and varied textures.

Amidst the bustling heat of the market, we found

ourselves unexpectedly swept into a whirlwind of commotion and chaos. From a distance, we came to a standstill, our eyes drawn toward the epicenter of the commotion. What could provoke such fervor? A palpable tension hung in the air. We stood there, merely spectators in this unfolding drama, our curiosity amplified, and our senses heightened.

The waves of people surged toward the epicenter, converging from every nook and cranny of the market. Their urgency was unmistakable. The throng surged; strangers brushed against one another, their gazes fixed ahead, their anticipation and curiosity amplified.

As the crowd thickened, a profound tension hung in the air. We stretched our necks, yearning for a glimpse of the front, where the focal point of this human frenzy lay.

Remarkably, as we strained to peer through the throngs of people, an inexplicable pathway suddenly opened before us. The crowd, a once-unified throng, parted, cleaving onto two sides, thus creating an open pathway.

In the heart of the bustling market, an extraordinary scene captured our attention. Amidst the chaos, two women of considerable build sat with a silent air of calmness. Their dark, radiant skin appeared to shimmer as if kissed by the sunlight.

Perched on short-legged stools, unpretentious yet robust, they were elevated a mere twelve to fourteen inches from the ground. These humble seats, though low, were remarkably sturdy. Flanking each woman were baskets brimming with the vibrant bounty of market life itself—fruits and vegetables in a medley of flavors and textures.

Both women sat with their legs outstretched before them, their pleated skirts cascading in a vibrant array of colors down to their ankles. From beneath these lively folds, the sight of little black ballerina shoes peeked out, adding a touch of whimsical contrast to their attire.

Nestled between these two women was a man, perched like a bird upon a lofty stool. His thin frame and unusually pale complexion stood in stark contrast to the colorful market scene, making him a focal point amidst the bustling environment. His attire, too, was a nod to a bygone era—an echo of the old world amidst modern chaos.

However, it was the intricate details of his ensemble that truly captured our attention. From the neck down, he was clad entirely in white. His shoes, with elongated points that curled upward, were adorned with small gold bells at their tips. His straight-legged pants, meticulously tailored, featured symmetrical seams that ran down each leg, ending just above the heel.

He wore an oversized shirt with sleeves billowing like sails in the wind, neatly tucked into his trousers at the waist. This ensemble was cinched with a wide belt, its gold surface gleaming in a flamboyant display of wealth and power.

Suddenly, standing upright and commanding, he began addressing the throngs of people. His voice echoed through the air, laden with audacious proclamations of his extraordinary psychic expertise and supernatural authority. His words, masterfully woven into a mesmerizing tapestry of self-assured confidence, unabashed pride, and unapologetic arrogance, held the crowd captive. His speech was a potent cocktail that intoxicated the listeners, leaving them in awe of his claimed supremacy.

Then, as if to lend credence to his audacious declaration, he embarked on a captivating display of his abilities. He began to single out individuals from the sea of faces in the crowd, their expressions a canvas of anxiety intermingled with anticipation. In that electrifying moment, the market's vibrant loudness fell into a hushed silence.

As the anxious souls stepped into the spotlight, their arms outstretched, he began to read their palms. His fingers danced over the lines of their hands, tracing the roadmap of their lives etched in their skin. He then purported to unveil their future, his words painting vivid pictures of what lay ahead. The crowd, caught in a state of awe and suspense, held their collective breath, their hearts beating in rhythm with the unfolding spectacle. The market was no longer just a marketplace; it had transformed into a theater of the uncanny, with every soul playing their part in this unexpected drama.

My mother and I stood on the periphery, our eyes riveted to the unfolding spectacle. Our skepticism was evident as we observed his uncanny charm and the influence he wielded over the crowd. The crowd, in turn, was utterly entranced, captivated by his magnetic presence and staged antics.

They hung onto his every word, their attention unwavering, as if each syllable were a precious gem. Each gesture drew them deeper into his sphere of influence, their skepticism dissolving under the warmth of his charisma. It was a remarkable demonstration of the power of persuasion. I cautioned those around me, "Do not be deceived by his theatrics."

As Mother and I prepared to depart, he caught a fleeting glimpse of us from the corner of his eye. "Wait!" he called out, beckoning us forward with a commanding gesture. The realization dawned on us that we had unwittingly captured his attention, and his motions grew increasingly insistent.

We could sense the challenge he was preparing to lay before us. His gaze, sharp and penetrating, coupled with the icy timbre of his voice, ignited a spark of indignation within us. Yet, we stood our ground, resolutely defiant and unyielding. We refused to be mere pawns in his elaborate game. With a shared look of defiance, we turned on our heels and walked away, our steps echoing with the resolve to chart our own course, undeterred by his attempts to sway us.

"Wait," he cried out again, "Why are you running away? Are you afraid?" His voice, laced with malevolence, tore through the air once more, his aggression toward us bordering on brazen disrespect. The marketgoers, too, felt the tension. They shifted uneasily, their gazes darting like nervous sparrows between him and us as we continued our departure. His audacity had disrupted the rhythm of the marketplace, but we remained steadfast, leaving the scene with our heads held high as he continued to call out to us.

Then, in a moment of divine inspiration, a surge of righteous indignation welled up within me. With a voice resonating with the power of conviction, I cried out, "Satan, I rebuke you in the Name of Jesus." My words echoed through the market, a shout that pierced the usual din.

The crowd, momentarily stunned into silence, was thrown into a state of confusion. They dispersed swiftly and without hesitation. Soon, the once-bustling marketplace was eerily empty, save for the man and the two large women who sat like silent sentinels at his sides.

His dominion, once seemingly unshakeable, crumbled before our eyes. The crowd, previously under his sway, was now liberated from his control. His iron-like grip on the marketplace was broken, and the people were free, leaving behind only the echoes of my proclamation and the remnants of his shattered authority.

Overwhelmed by frustration, he stooped low, tightly

gripping his possessions before hastily retreating. In a final act of defiance, he swiveled around, directing a hardened, icy stare toward us that seemed to cut through the air like a blade. His gaze, as cold and unyielding as a winter storm, felt as if it were piercing the very core of my being. I was acutely aware that this confrontation was merely a skirmish in a war that was far from over.

Finally, Mother and I managed to extricate ourselves from the bustling market, embarking on our journey back home. There was a sense of minor triumph in the air, a small victory in an ongoing battle. Yet, my spirit was far from at peace. I was troubled, knowing that this issue was merely dormant for a little while, but not resolved. It was a specter that would undoubtedly resurface, casting a long shadow over our future encounters.

At home later that evening, I vividly recall, in the dream, our family convening in the dining room, a space dominated by a grand window. From our vantage point on the second floor, we had a clear view of the street below. As we nestled into our seats, a tapping sound punctuated the silence—a rhythmic pattern that was both persistent and unsettling. The room fell into a hush, the air thick with anticipation.

The source of the sound was someone at street level, hurling small stones at our window with urgent and demanding persistence. It was a call for attention that could not be ignored. Compelled to investigate, I rose from my chair and crossed the room, each step echoing my growing apprehension. A sense of foreboding washed over me, a gut feeling that something was awry.

As I found myself peering through the window, my eyes met the cold gaze of the psychic—the man shrouded in mystery who had earlier shattered our tranquility at the bustling market. There he was, standing defiantly, his hand rhythmically launching small stones that clattered against the glass. A chill ran down my spine as I realized the truth of my earlier intuition—this confrontation, this silent war, was far from over.

Caught off guard, I wondered how he knew our address. Had he followed us home? My mind raced with questions.

Then, a woman emerged from behind him and stood a few steps ahead of him. Her eyes, a piercing shade of bluish green, held an unsettling intensity. No matter where I turned, I found myself unable to escape her intense gaze; her lips held a sinister smile that gave me cause for concern. Despite her undeniable beauty, there was an ominous aura surrounding her, an intense sense of wickedness and evil that was impossible to ignore.

Suddenly, without a hint of forewarning, she began to levitate, rising three to four feet above the ground. Her body remained suspended in midair, defying gravity. As she rose, our eyes locked in a silent battle of the will. Her gaze was unwavering, filled with a chilling determination. Everything around us seemed to hold its breath at that very moment in time.

A wave of malicious, obnoxious evil radiated from her very being, wrapping the surroundings in a cloak of chilling dread that was impossible to ignore. It was as if the air itself had turned icy. An instinctive realization dawned upon me; a truth, undeniable and profound, resonating deep within the recesses of my spirit. I was staring into the face of a witch, a sorcerer, an individual who had willingly surrendered herself to the dark arts, who was resolute and committed to her god, the devil.

Her presence was far from mere coincidence; she had

deliberately sought me out, her intentions seething with vengeance. This was no random encounter; it was a calculated move, a chess game in the grand scheme of darkness. Her motivation was fueled by a burning desire for retribution, a response to the disruption I had caused to her servant's deceitful dealings earlier that day at the marketplace and their desire to deceive the masses into serving the same god they were serving.

I cried out, "The blood of Jesus be against you!" My voice echoed into the night, a desperate plea for divine intervention. Yet, unlike the previous encounter where my words had held power, this time, they seemed to dissolve into thin air, falling on deaf ears.

Her sinister smile remained untouched and unscathed. It was as if my words had lost their potency. Her cold and cruel smile lingered on; it was a silent ridicule of my faith. But despite setbacks, I knew that my faith was unshaken, my resolve unbroken. For I knew the ultimate victory belonged to God, and no amount of darkness could extinguish it.

My thoughts gravitated toward the profound narrative found in the Book of Daniel, Chapter Three. This chapter recounts the unwavering faith of four Hebrew youths—Shadrach, Meshach, Abednego, and Daniel. Despite facing extreme adversity under the reign of King Nebuchadnezzar of Babylon, their faith remained unshaken. Shadrach, Meshach, and Abednego stood resolute even when confronted with the threat of a fiery furnace, while Daniel later faced the den of lions and emerged unscathed. Their steadfastness serves as a powerful witness to the strength of faith and conviction.

The four young men were assigned Babylonian names by the prince of the eunuchs: Daniel was renamed

Belteshazzar, Hananiah became Shadrach, Mishael was called Meshach, and Azariah was known as Abednego. These youths were among the residents of Jerusalem who were captured by Nebuchadnezzar, the formidable King of Babylon, during the third year of Jehoiakim's rule as king of Judah, who was also taken captive and exiled to Babylon.

Despite their captivity, Daniel, Hananiah, Mishael, and Azariah remained steadfast in their devotion to the Living God, refusing to partake in the food served at the King's table. This food was offered to the children of Jehoiakim's lineage, as well as to children of princes—youths without blemish, skilled in wisdom, knowledgeable, well-favored, and understanding of science. These children were to be made proficient in learning the language of the Chaldeans.

In all the province of King Nebuchadnezzar, there were none like these four young men—Daniel, Hananiah, Mishael, and Azariah—whom the King found to be ten times better in all matters of wisdom and understanding than all the magicians, astrologers, and soothsayers that served in his kingdom. Consequently, he placed them in positions of authority within his realm.

When King Nebuchadnezzar seized Judah, he brought back portions of the sacred vessels from the house of God and transported them to the land of Shinar, to the temple of his god. The remaining sacred vessels were placed in the treasure house of his deity. For Nebuchadnezzar, this act was a glaring indication of his powerful conquest and his total disregard for the sanctity of these holy artifacts.

The Impertinent Proclamation

With all power under his hand, King Nebuchadnezzar constructed a colossal image of gold, towering at a height of threescore cubits and a breadth of six cubits (approximately 90 feet high by 10.5 feet wide). This imposing figure was erected in the expansive plain of Dura, located in the province of Babylon.

Subsequently, King Nebuchadnezzar summoned the princes, governors, captains, judges, treasurers, counselors, sheriffs, and all provincial rulers to attend the dedication of the image he had commissioned. These dignitaries, representing the breadth and depth of the kingdom, convened for the dedication ceremony, standing in awe before the towering golden image that Nebuchadnezzar had established.

A proclaimer then announced in a loud voice, commanding all people, nations, and languages that upon hearing the cornet, flute, harp, sackbut, psaltery, dulcimer, and all kinds of music, they were to prostrate themselves and worship the golden image that King Nebuchadnezzar had set up. The proclamation carried a dire warning: Any who failed to fall and worship the golden image would be cast into the midst of a burning, fiery furnace within the hour.

Thus, when the music played, and the people, nations, and languages heard the symphony of the cornet, flute, harp, sackbut, psaltery, and all kinds of music, they fell and worshipped the golden image that King Nebuchadnezzar had set up, complying with the king's decree in a display of obedience out of fear.

During this period, certain Chaldeans, who served as court astronomers, sorcerers, and magicians under King Nebuchadnezzar, approached the king with accusations against specific Jews appointed to oversee the province of Babylon. These Jews were Shadrach, Meshach, and Abednego, known for their unwavering devotion to the

Living God rather than the deities worshipped by the Babylonian kingdom. Motivated by jealousy and a desire to undermine their positions, the Chaldeans accused Shadrach, Meshach, and Abednego of defying the king's decree.

This decree mandated that all subjects must bow down and worship the golden image whenever the music is played. The Chaldeans reminded the king of the severe punishment outlined in his decree: anyone who failed to comply would be cast into a blazing, fiery furnace.

Enraged by the disobedience of these Hebrew officials, Nebuchadnezzar commanded that the young men be brought before him:

> 13 *Then Nebuchadnezzar in his rage and fury commanded to bring Shadrach, Meshach, and Abednego. Then they brought these men before the king.*
>
> 14 *Nebuchadnezzar spake and said unto them, Is it true, O Shadrach, Meshach, and Abednego, do not ye serve my gods, nor worship the golden image which I have set up?*
>
> **15** *Now if ye be ready that at what time ye hear the sound of the cornet, flute, harp, sackbut, psaltery, and dulcimer, and all kinds of musick, ye fall down and worship the image which I have made; well: but if ye worship not, ye shall be cast the same hour into the midst of a burning fiery furnace; and who is that God that shall deliver you out of my hands?*
>
> — DANIEL 3:13-14

Shadrach, Meshach, and Abednego answered the king with unwavering faith and conviction, saying:

> *[16] O Nebuchadnezzar, we are not careful to answer thee in this matter. [17] If it be so, our God whom we serve is able to deliver us from the burning fiery furnace, and he will deliver us out of thine hand, O king. [18] But if not, be it known unto thee, O king, that we will not serve thy gods, nor worship the golden image which thou hast set up.*
>
> — DANIEL 3:16-18

Then Nebuchadnezzar, full of fury and the form of his visage was changed against them, commanded that the furnace be heated seven times hotter than its normal temperature. He then commanded the mightiest men in his army to bind Shadrach, Meshach, and Abednego and cast them into the burning fiery furnace.

These Hebrew men were bound in their coats, trousers, hats, and other garments and cast alive into the burning fiery furnace. Due to the urgency of the king's command and the extreme heat, the flames consumed the soldiers who oversaw Shadrach, Meshach, and Abednego.

As the king watched with anticipation, expecting the men to be consumed by the flames, he turned to his counselors and exclaimed:

> *[24] Then Nebuchadnezzar the king was astonished, and rose up in haste, and spake, and said unto his counsellors, Did not we cast three men bound into the midst of the fire? They answered and said unto the king, True, O king.*
>
> *[25] He answered and said, Lo, I see four men loose, walking in the midst of the fire, and they have no hurt; and the form of the fourth is like the Son of God.*
>
> — DANIEL 3:24-25

Nebuchadnezzar recognizes the Power of the One True and Living God

26 *Then Nebuchadnezzar came near to the mouth of the burning fiery furnace, and spake, and said, Shadrach, Meshach, and Abednego, ye servants of the most high God, come forth, and come hither. Then Shadrach, Meshach, and Abednego, came forth of the midst of the fire.*

27 *And the princes, governors, and captains, and the king's counsellors, being gathered together, saw these men, upon whose bodies the fire had no power, nor was an hair of their head singed, neither were their coats changed, nor the smell of fire had passed on them.*

28 *Then Nebuchadnezzar spake, and said, Blessed be the God of Shadrach, Meshach, and Abednego, who hath sent his angel, and delivered his servants that trusted in him, and have changed the king's word, and yielded their bodies, that they might not serve nor worship any god, except their own God.*

29 *Therefore I make a decree, That every people, nation, and language, which speak any thing amiss against the God of Shadrach, Meshach, and Abednego, shall be cut in pieces, and their houses shall be made a dunghill: because there is no other God that can deliver after this sort.*

30 *Then the king promoted Shadrach, Meshach, and Abednego, in the province of Babylon.*

Many people believe that colossal structures are relics of a bygone era, but this is not entirely accurate. Across the globe, modern nations continue to construct monumental statues that stand as testaments to the worship of their deities based on their cultural and historical heritage. [1]Some of the most notable examples include:

1. **Statue of Unity**: Located in the Narmada River, Gujarat, India, this statue is the world's tallest, standing at 597 feet. It honors India's first Deputy Prime Minister, Sardar Vallabhbhai Patel.
2. **Spring Temple Buddha**: Situated in Lushan County, Henan, China, this statue stands at 420 feet and is one of the tallest statues in the world.
3. **Laykyun Sekkya**: Found in Khatakan Taung, Myanmar, this statue stands at 380 feet and is a significant landmark in the region.
4. **Statue of Belief - Vishwas Swaroopam**: Located in Nathdwara, Rajasthan, India, this statue stands at 348 feet and is a recent addition to India's monumental structures.
5. **Statue - Ushiku Daibutsu**: Situated in Ushiku, Ibaraki Prefecture, Japan, this statue stands at 330 feet and is a prominent symbol of Japanese culture.
6. **Statue - Sendai Daikannon**: Located in Sendai, Miyagi Prefecture, Japan, this statue stands at 330 feet and is one of the tallest statues in Japan.
7. **Statue - Guishan Guanyin**: Found in Weishan, Changsha, Hunan, China, this statue stands at 325 feet and is a revered figure in Chinese Buddhism.
8. **Statue - Great Buddha of Thailand**: Situated in Ang Thong Province, Thailand, this statue stands at 305 feet and is a significant religious monument.
9. **Statue - Kita no Miyako Park's Dai Kannon**: Located in Ashibetsu, Hokkaido, Japan, this

statue stands at 289 feet and is a notable landmark in the region.

10. **Statue - Mother of All Asia-Tower of Peace**: Found in the Philippines, this statue stands at 289 feet and symbolizes peace and unity.

[1]**Source: Adda247 Current Affairs: "Top 10 Tallest Statues in The World"**

Like the Hebrew young men, my faith remained unshaken, knowing that ultimate victory belongs to God and no darkness could extinguish it.

The Shed Blood of Jesus Christ Cleanses

At that moment, a profound realization dawned upon me. The blood of Jesus was not a weapon to wield against evil but a divine cleansing power bestowed upon us by our Lord Jesus Christ. It sanctifies us, washing away our sins, purifying us from within, and making us whole and holy in His sight. The shed blood of Jesus Christ further cleanses us from all unrighteousness, making us worthy to stand in His presence.

I realized my words had been incorrect; I was not to command, "The blood of Jesus be against you, Satan." Because I understood that the shed blood of the Lord Jesus Christ is a testament to His love and sacrifice for us and symbolizes redemption and renewal, and not a tool of rebuke and condemnation. It is a true reminder of His mercy, forgiveness, and His desire for us to be cleansed and made new when we confess our sins.

The correct invocation emerged from the depths of my faith, echoing with newfound clarity: "Satan, I rebuke you in the Name of Jesus." This is the true spiritual command, a divine rebuke against the forces of darkness, and a testament to the supreme authority of the Lord Jesus Christ. We must understand that there is no other name under heaven given among men whereby we must be saved.

> [10] *Be it known unto you all, and to all the people of Israel, that by the name of Jesus Christ of Nazareth, whom ye crucified, whom God raised from the dead, even by him doth this man stand here before you whole.* [11] *This is the stone which was set at nought of you builders, which is become the head of the corner.* [12] *Neither is there salvation in any other: for there is none other name under heaven given among men, whereby we must be saved.*
>
> — ACTS 4:10-12

> [9]*Wherefore God also hath highly exalted him, and given him a name which is above every name:* [10]*That at the name of Jesus every knee should bow, of things in heaven, and things in earth, and things under the earth;* [11]*And that every tongue should confess that Jesus Christ is Lord, to the glory of God the Father.*
>
> — PHILIPPIANS 2:9-10

> [11] *For it is written, As I live, saith the Lord, every knee shall bow to me, and every tongue shall confess to God.*
>
> — ROMANS 14:11

As those words left my lips, I sensed a tangible shift in the atmosphere. Then, as if swallowed by the night, both she and the man vanished into thin air without a trace. It was as if reality blinked, leaving nothing but the echo of their presence.

Suddenly, I was jolted awake! The remnants of the dream remained steadfast in my memory. A stark realization hit me—the Blood of Jesus Christ cannot cleanse the devil, fallen angels, or demons, nor can they receive the gift of sin's forgiveness. The Lord Jesus Christ did not come to earth to die on the cross for the devil, the fallen angels, or the malevolent spirits. His sacrifice was for mankind so that *"whosoever believes in Him should not perish but have eternal life."*

> [16] *For God so loved the world, that he gave his only begotten Son, that whosoever believeth in him should not perish, but have everlasting life.* [17] *For God sent not his Son into the world to condemn the world; but that the world through him might be saved.* [18] *He that believeth on him is not condemned: but he that believeth not is condemned already, because he hath not believed in the name of the only begotten Son of God.* [19]*And this is the condemnation, that light is come into the world, and men loved darkness rather than light because their deeds were evil.*
>
> — John 3:16-19

There is absolutely no salvation or hope for the devil; he knows he is forever lost. In stark contrast, humanity, as long as the breath of life fills their lungs, retains the hope of receiving forgiveness for their sins and the promise of eternal life in heaven with the Father and His Son. This is the divine truth.

The devil is acutely aware of this immutable fact, and it

is a truth he is powerless to change. His defeat is inevitable, and there is absolutely nothing he can do to alter his doomed fate. Given this reality, it is perplexing why some people still choose to serve him.

> [35] *Who shall separate us from the love of Christ? shall tribulation, or distress, or persecution, or famine, or nakedness, or peril, or sword?*
>
> [36] *As it is written, For thy sake we are killed all the day long; we are accounted as sheep for the slaughter.*
>
> [37] *Nay, in all these things we are more than conquerors through him that loved us.*
>
> [38] *For I am persuaded, that neither death, nor life, nor angels, nor principalities, nor powers, nor things present, nor things to come,*
>
> [39] *Nor height, nor depth, nor any other creature, shall be able to separate us from the love of God, which is in Christ Jesus our Lord. Amen!*
>
> — ROMANS 8:35-37

Chapter 11

Ancient Demonic Spirits

In an open vision, I found myself in spirit form within an old antique shop, facing the front entry door. The floor beneath my feet, with its dark wood, worn and weathered, bore witness to countless footsteps that had traversed its surface over the years.

In a dimly lit corner of the shop, two antiquated and imposing thrones stood in silent majesty. The upholstery, though faded, still whispered of its former grandeur, speaking of luxury and prestige. Their red velvet seats and backrests, once symbols of opulence and regality, now bore the weight of centuries. These striking seats appeared as relics from an era of chivalry and romance, a time when knights fought valiantly, minstrels sang tales of heroism, and feasts filled the great halls of grand castles. The thrones were far more than mere pieces of furniture; they were symbols of power and authority, reserved for the distinguished presence of kings, queens, and nobility from centuries past.

As I stood there amid the antique shop, the air grew

dense with an uncanny charge. The shop itself was a labyrinth of history, filled with relics and artifacts from bygone eras. Each item seemed to whisper stories of the past, creating an atmosphere that was both strange and eerie. The dim lighting cast long shadows, adding to the shop's mysterious allure.

It was at this moment that I became cognizant of two mysterious figures entering the shop. These individuals were shrouded in an aura of malevolence, their countenances and presence carried a peculiar weight, stirring within me a growing sense of unease and disdain. The atmosphere darkened around them as I watched them move through the shop with unsettling grace.

I found myself observing them in hushed silence, my gaze drawn to their antiquated attire and demeanor. The first man was garbed in the attire of a Viking warrior. His stature was not particularly imposing, standing at an average height, yet there was an undeniable presence about him, a powerful sense of evil. Atop his head sat a Viking helmet, its surface gleaming with a metallic sheen. The helmet, with its curved horns, was a symbol of the Viking warriors of ancient times.

The second man, noticeably shorter in stature, made his entrance into the store simultaneously with the first but maintained a few steps distance behind him. His distance was a result of his position, as if in a display of submissiveness or strategic respect.

With a sense of purpose, they began to move. Their footsteps moved swiftly across the ancient floor, yet they did not once glance in my direction. As I stood there, a silent observer, I was struck by a sudden realization: I was invisible to them.

Their unwavering focus was intensely fixed upon two

artifacts: the ancient thrones, shrouded in mystery and age, standing in the far corner of the old antique shop. Like moths drawn to a flame, the men were irresistibly captivated by these relics, consumed by the enigmatic allure of the thrones. The intricate craftsmanship and the aura of forgotten royalty emanating from the thrones seemed to compel the men to delve deeper into the secrets they held. Each detail, from the worn velvet cushions to the ornate carvings, whispered tales of a period long past.

In that profound moment, the Spirit of the Lord spoke to me. His voice, a harmonious blend of authority and gentleness, resonated through the corridors of my soul, sending a chill down my spine. The words He uttered were both powerful and unsettling: *"ANCIENT DEMONIC SPIRITS."*

What I beheld before me were no ordinary men. Their forms, though appearing to be cloaked in flesh and bone, were malevolent spirits from an era long past. This open vision lingered in my mind, raising questions that gnawed at my soul. Why had they come? Why were they drawn to the time-worn ancient thrones that sat dormant in the dimly lit corners of the antiquarian shop? Could it be that these malevolent dark spirits once held sway over the rulers, the monarchs who presided over these seats of power?

Had their dark whispers shaped the destinies of kingdoms and steered the course of empires, nations, and peoples against the True and Living God in a bygone epoch?

Were they the unseen puppeteers, their strings pulling at the course of history, bending it to their dark will?

As many of you are aware, the demons of ages past are the very same forces that continue to influence and shape our society today, albeit masquerading under a myriad of different names or labels. These entities, once worshipped and revered by ancient civilizations, persist in their influence in the contemporary world, although shrouded or cloaked in fresh disguises and revered and idolized by a multitude of cultures spanning the globe. This is a stark and sobering truth we must confront.

We inhabit a world marred by imperfection, and throughout the chronicles of history, the accounts of the devil, fallen angels, and demons have been woven into its fabric. Their sinister purpose endures even as their identities and manifestations morph with the relentless passage of time.

Their tales, as old as time itself, have been recounted and passed down through generations, a chilling testament to their persistent presence in our world. Their purpose and plan remain as ominous as ever. This is the somber reality of our existence in this fallen world.

These wicked forces are relentless in their pursuit, seeking to shape the very essence of humanity—our designs, fashions, cultures, and who we are. Their goal remains unchanged: to divert humanity's gaze away from God's path and ensnare hearts in the web of darkness.

The devil, the ancient adversary, is a cunning conspirator and schemer. He stands in the shadows of the authorities, his battlefield extending beyond the physical realm to infiltrate the corridors of power. From the lofty heights of presidents, kings, and queens to governors, mayors, judges, political figures, leaders, organizations, media, artists, athletes, and sports personnel—anyone with great influence.

When the enemy cannot directly influence a person in authority, he strategically places individuals around them to obstruct that leader from discovering the truth, creating a barrier that prevents the masses from hearing God's Truth or anyone who speaks it.

Spiritual discernment is crucial in recognizing these tactics. It involves a heightened awareness and sensitivity to the spiritual realm, allowing one to perceive the subtle influences and deceptions at play. Discernment enables individuals to see beyond the surface and identify the true nature of situations and people. It is a gift that requires constant nurturing through prayer, and the studying God's Word. However, with many churches shunning the Holy Spirit of God in their services, discernment becomes skewed and less effective.

In a world filled with distractions and falsehoods, the precious Holy Spirit illuminates the path to righteousness and integrity.

Deception by the enemy is vividly chronicled in the Book of Acts of the Apostles, Chapter 13, Verses 6–12.

On their missionary journey, Barnabas and Saul traversed the country of Cyprus, until they arrived at Paphos. There they found a certain sorcerer, a false prophet, a Jew, whose name was Bar-Jesus. He was with the deputy of the country, a man by the name of Sergius Paulus, a prudent man. The deputy, intrigued by Barnabas and Saul's teachings, called for them, expressing his desire to hear the word of God.

However, Elymas, also known as Bar-Jesus, the sorcerer (which is his name by interpretation), stood in their way, attempting to turn the deputy, his superior, away from the faith. Then Saul, also known as Paul, filled with the Holy Spirit, fixed a stern gaze on Elymas and declared, [10] *Oh, full of all deceit and all mischief, you child of the devil, enemy of all righteousness, will you not cease to pervert the right ways of the Lord? And now, behold, the hand of the Lord is upon you, and you shall be blind, not seeing the sun for a season.* (Acts 13:10). Immediately, a mist and a darkness (blindness) fell upon him, and he went about seeking someone to lead him by the hand.

Sergius Paulus, the deputy, upon witnessing this, was astounded by the doctrine of the Lord and believed in their teachings, his faith ignited by the divine intervention he had witnessed.

Without a doubt, within the ceaseless turmoil of this timeless struggle, there exists a promise of redemption—a day when the culmination of this age-old conflict will see the forces of evil cast into the abyss, ignited by fire and brimstone, which will become their everlasting prison, where they shall endure an eternity of retribution. It is a day foretold, a day of virtue over wickedness that will herald the triumph of light over darkness, good over evil, and righteousness over malevolence.

Chapter 12

The Tragedy of Blind Allegiance

This dream unfolded from 2015 to 2016. In this vivid dream, I found myself in spirit form, standing in a large church located in Johannesburg, South Africa. I was not on the platform but positioned at the front of the church, slightly to the side, my gaze directed toward the throngs of people who made up the congregation. The carpet beneath my feet was a vibrant shade of red.

Standing a few feet away from me to my right was the pastor, the shepherd of the flock. His eyes methodically swept over the audience, moving his head from left to right as if he were in search of someone or something. The pastor's presence was commanding, and the crowd looked both anxiously and excitedly toward him. Their anticipation was intense as they hoped to attract his attention.

They came from far and near, from distant lands and across the oceans. They arrived with hope in their hearts, their finances, and pictures of loved ones for whom they were desperately praying. Faces were filled with a mix of hope and desperation, yearning for him to speak a word in their lives or lay his hands upon them for a miracle. The air was thick with expectation, each person silently praying to be the one chosen for a divine encounter.

Suddenly, his gaze locked with mine. A wave of concern washed over me, fearing that he might rebuke me or have me removed by his security.

His eyes captured my attention; they were dark and wide. The intensity of his gaze was both unsettling and disturbing, as if he could peer into the deepest recesses of my being despite knowing that he could not. The sheer force of his stare left me feeling exposed and vulnerable, as though every hidden thought and emotion were laid bare before him.

However, to my utter astonishment, even though our eyes met in a shared stare, he was unable to see me. I was invisible to him, a presence unseen amid the congregation. This unexpected revelation left me in a state of respite.

Although in the dream he appeared charming, sincere and exuded undeniable charisma, devoted to serving the Almighty God, I pondered, *"If only the congregation could understand that he is a false prophet, one whose teachings are fabricated and deceptive. He does not represent the Lord God, for the Spirit of the Lord God is not present in him nor this sanctuary."*

Beneath his gaze, I discerned his deep involvement in Satanism, the belief in the worship of Satan, as well as witchcraft and the occult, all of which are biblically forbidden. Satan is his god, the one to whom he has pledged his allegiance. What is worse, a significant number of pastors, ministers, and other leaders were cognizant of this unsettling fact because they, too, were involved in the same dark cult. Despite this, they persisted in their involvement in his elaborate charade. They were not merely passive accomplices in this complex web of deceit but were generously compensated financially for their complicity.

Their willingness to turn a blind eye and participate in such darkness for material gain and praise is a stark reminder of the pervasive influence of evil and the moral decay that has infiltrated even the most sacred institutions, it also underscores the vulnerability of human nature to corruption and the seductive power of wealth and recognition.

The depths of their deception were profound, as they skillfully masked their true intentions behind a façade of piety and righteousness. They manipulated the trust and faith of their congregations, exploiting their spiritual authority to further their own nefarious agendas.

As I shifted my gaze towards the audience, the musicians and singers were enthralling them with their riveting performance. The audience was ensnared in a state of blissful oblivion, swallowing wholeheartedly everything that was served to them without a hint of skepticism.

They adored their leader and held him in the highest regard, awestruck by his brazen display of fabricated miracles. Their hearts were shrouded in a veil of blindness and ignorance, preventing them from discerning the truth behind the spectacle. This veil led them further and deeper into illusion, making them vulnerable to manipulation and deceit.

I awoke from the dream in a state of profound disturbance. The individual I had seen was a highly revered pastor and prophet in Africa. I wondered, *"Who could I confide in about this dream? Who would believe me?"* This revelation left me grappling with a deep sense of unease and a heavy burden of knowledge that was difficult to bear.

The weight of this vision pressed upon my spirit, leaving me in a state of inner turmoil.

My mind traveled back to the haunting memory of the cult leader who orchestrated the Jonestown Massacre in 1978. Jim Jones, the self-proclaimed messiah of the Peoples Temple, led over 900 of his followers to commit mass suicide in Jonestown, Guyana, after promising them a utopia in the jungles of South America. His followers' blind allegiance to him and his teachings resulted in one of the most tragic mass suicides in history. This false leader, born in Indiana, U.S., led his followers away from the safety of their families to a distant land they knew very little about.

Jones's ability to manipulate and control his congregation, leading them to such a devastating end, underscores the importance of discernment and vigilance in the face of deceptive influences. The Jonestown Massacre remains a somber testament to the destructive power of false prophets and the catastrophic consequences of blind allegiance.

The parallels between the revered pastor/prophet in my dream and Jim Jones were unsettling. Both wielded immense influence over their followers, who placed unwavering trust in their leadership. The thought of such blind allegiance and the potential for manipulation and harm weighed heavily on my heart.

As I pondered the significance of the dream, I felt an urgent need to share it with other trusted leaders. The burden of this revelation was too great to bear alone. I knew that only through prayer and seeking God's wisdom could I find clarity and direction.

In my quest for understanding, I was reminded of the importance of discernment and vigilance in matters of faith. Many people are being misled by those pretending to be prophets whose gifts are not from God but from hell. Jesus boldly proclaimed to many masquerading as prophets that He did not know them, as stated in Matthew 7:21-23: [21] *Not every one that saith unto me, 'Lord, Lord, shall enter into the kingdom of heaven; but he that doeth the will of my Father which is in heaven.* [22] *Many will say to me in that day, Lord, Lord, have we not prophesied in thy name? and in thy name have cast out devils? and in thy name done many wonderful works?* [23] *And then will I profess unto them, I never knew you: depart from me, ye that work iniquity.*

The safety and wisdom found in a multitude of counselors, as stated in Proverbs 11:14, is invaluable in navigating these spiritual challenges.

> [14] *"Where no counsel is, the people fall: but in the multitude of counsellors there is safety."*

Chapter 13

Shorts

A FATEFUL ENCOUNTER IN NEW YORK CITY

After a vocal training session in New York City, my daughter and I began our journey towards Penn Station. She had asked me to accompany her, knowing the time would be late following the rehearsal. It was around ten-thirty in the evening, early October, and the city had settled into a quiet lull. The shops were closed, their lights extinguished, casting long shadows on the deserted streets.

As we walked briskly, my daughter a few steps ahead, I noticed a woman standing in the doorway of a closed shop. She wore a button-up denim dress that reached just below her thigh. Hearing our footsteps, she leaned forward, her eyes searching the darkness to identify us.

In that fleeting moment, I recognized her as a "woman of the night." A wave of empathy washed over me as I pondered the circumstances that had led her to this point. It was clear to me that she did not belong there and that her presence was not by choice. I felt a profound burden for her, sensing the weight of her plight and the unseen forces that had driven her to such a life.

Suddenly, the Spirit of the Lord spoke expressly to me, saying, *"I WANT YOU TO SPEAK THE FOLLOWING WORDS TO HER. WHEN YOU DO, KEEP YOUR FACE FORWARD AS A FLINT. DO NOT TURN YOUR HEAD TO LOOK AT HER. ONLY SPEAK THAT WHICH I GIVE YOU TO SPEAK; SPEAK ONLY THE WORDS I GIVE YOU."*

At that moment, I felt a profound mix of emotions. There was a deep sense of compassion and sorrow for the woman standing in the doorway. My heart ached for her, knowing that she was likely in a situation beyond her control. I felt an overwhelming burden for her well-being, as if my heart was silently weeping for her plight.

At the same time, I felt an intense sense of urgency and responsibility when the Spirit of the Lord spoke to me. There was a clear directive to deliver a message, and I felt a mixture of reverence and determination to follow through with what I was being asked to do. The instruction to keep my face forward and speak only the words given to me added a layer of solemnity and focus to the moment.

As I drew closer to the woman, I quickly glanced at her, making brief eye contact without turning my head. Then, with a surge of conviction, I cried out what the Spirit of the Lord instructed me to say: *"GOD IS ABLE; GOD IS ABLE!"* and continued walking. She stood there in silent surprise, motionless and unresponsive.

As I walked by, a man unexpectedly emerged from the shadows across the street. He had been lurking in the doorway of a closed shop, watching the woman, my daughter, and me, unbeknownst to us. My daughter was completely unaware of the message the Spirit of the Lord had imparted to me. The man then shouted from across the street, "Good evening, ma'am, how are you?"

At that moment, I realized he was her pimp and had been watching us before I noticed! According to the Merriam-Webster Dictionary, a pimp is defined as "a criminal who is associated with, usually exerts control over, and lives off the earnings of one or more prostitutes."

A wave of resentment and anger surged within me upon hearing his salutation, and I chose to ignore him. My daughter, however, hearing his greeting, turned in surprise and looked back at me, asking, "Mum, didn't you hear the man speaking to you?"

I responded to him immediately, saying, "Good evening, I'm fine, thank you!" and continued walking.

He then yelled out, "Have a good evening."

This incident of being watched reminded me of another unsettling experience that occurred one night at a beach where my family and friends had gathered for a celebration and to dine at one of the many waterfront restaurants.

As we enjoyed the evening, I became aware of a group of young women sitting separately on the beach, as if waiting for someone. Sensing that something might be wrong, I approached two of the young ladies and asked if they were okay, if they were in trouble, and if they felt safe. They carefully looked around and, in broken English, told me they were from Poland and assured me they were okay.

Just then, I happened to turn my head and noticed a man standing in the doorway of a bustling restaurant, watching us intently. When the young women realized he had been observing them, they immediately stopped talking, jumped to their feet, and walked away from me in haste.

I looked at the man, and he looked back at me with a

smug expression as if amused and pleased with himself. I walked away but later discussed the incident with my relatives. What I found particularly disturbing was that there were people on the beach who ignored the situation.

When my daughter and I boarded the train that evening, I explained to her all that the Spirit of God had revealed to me and why I initially hesitated to respond to the individual when he called out to me. However, after hearing my daughter's words, I realized that if I had not responded, that poor woman might have faced his wrath.

That night, I found myself restless, unable to sleep after praying for her. I sensed she was innocently ensnared in a lifestyle she never chose, having fallen in love with a man she believed genuinely cared for her, only to be deceived and exploited for his own gain.

As I continued to pray, the Holy Spirit graciously revealed her desperate plea to the Lord for rescue. I believe she cried out, "Lord, if You can, please deliver me from this snare and this trap I'm caught in. Please set me free, Lord, please!" In my prayers, I envisioned the profound turmoil she must have endured—trapped in a life she never chose, her heart weighed down with despair and longing for freedom. The fear and hopelessness she experienced daily must have been overwhelming. Yet, amidst her suffering, there was a glimmer of hope, a desperate plea to God for deliverance.

That is why the Spirit of the Lord gave me those specific words for her. She would then know that the Lord God heard her and would deliver her and set her free. I can only depend on and believe that she was and has been delivered from the bondage of that wicked individual.

I fervently hope she felt a surge of comfort and

reassurance, knowing that God heard her cries that fateful evening in October.

THE DARK ALLEY

After a long and fulfilling church event, I boarded the last train of the evening, heading home. Upon reaching my stop, I descended the platform stairs to the street level. It was very late, and the streets were quiet.

Faced with two options, I could either take the long way home or walk through a shortcut alley that offered a clear-cut path for pedestrians. The alley was lined with thick green bushes, dense enough for someone to hide in without being noticed by passersby.

I chose the shortcut through the alley. As soon as I stepped in, a miraculous sight unfolded before me. In my spirit, I saw a band of angels who had encircled me, their swords and shields gleaming in their hands. Their bright, clear glow provided a profound sense of reassurance. With their heavenly protection, I continued to walk confidently, feeling an overwhelming sense of peace and security.

Unexpectedly, several feet ahead of me, I noticed that the man who had exited the train at the same time as I did and who had gone ahead of me into the alley was no longer in sight! It struck me as peculiar that he had managed to exit the alley so quickly.

Feeling a sense of trepidation, I continued to walk, glancing around me as I went. The alley was dimly lit, and the air was cool, carrying the faint scent of damp earth and foliage. As I approached the end of the alley, I suddenly heard whistling, intending to get my attention, coming from the bushes. The rustling of leaves added to the unsettling atmosphere.

Without turning my head to inquire, the Holy Spirit of God placed a song in my mouth, and at the top of my voice, I began to sing the praises of God. My voice echoed in the air, mingled with the sounds of night.

The man continued to call out to me as he hid in the bushes to the right of me. Within my spirit, as though I had eyes in the back of my head, I perceived him as a demonic spirit attempting to grab me from behind. However, the holy angels of God restrained him. I could feel their presence, a warm and protective aura surrounding me.

Once I was out of the alleyway and at a safe distance, I turned back to see, but no one was there. The street was silent, save for the distant sound of a passing car.

Two weeks later, my mother and I set off for work one morning, following our usual route through the alley to reach the train station. The morning air was crisp, and the sun had already risen. As the wind blew gently, we both caught a whiff of a foul smell in the air, a stark contrast to the fresh morning breeze.

That evening, as we made our way home, we were met with a shocking view. The alley was cordoned off with yellow tape, and police cars were everywhere. The flashing red and blue lights illuminated the scene, creating an unsettling atmosphere.

A crowd had gathered, held back by the tape, all straining to catch a glimpse of what had transpired, their faces a mix of curiosity and concern. The murmurs of the onlookers blended with the low hum of police radios, creating a subdued yet charged environment.

Cautiously, I approached an officer guarding the barrier and asked what was happening. He responded that the body of a young woman had been found in the bushes. The gravity of his words hung in the air, mingling with the lingering scent of decay.

My heart grieved deeply for the parents and family of that young woman whose life was tragically cut short. My prayers were filled with pleas for comfort and strength for her loved ones, hoping they would find solace amid their unimaginable grief.

"SEE, DIDN'T I MAKE A WAY OUT OF NO WAY?"

My family and I were on the verge of leaving the church we had faithfully served for five years. We were deeply troubled by what we perceived as ungodly actions within the ministry. In our distress, we sought the Lord through prayer and fasting, asking Him to guide us to a new church home. We were determined not to leave without first knowing where we would continue our fellowship.

As the situation at the ministry became increasingly unbearable and more congregants began to leave, we decided to meet with the pastor. We shared our heartfelt concerns and expressed that it was time for us to move on. This decision was incredibly difficult for us.

Despite our prayers, we still did not know where we would be fellowshipping next. One night, I had a profound dream: In the dream, I was running along the platform of a train station, pursued by six men intent on causing me harm. As I reached the end of the platform with nowhere else to go, a silent train pulled into the station, and its doors opened. I stopped running and took a deep breath of relief as I saw the conductor's hands glowing with a beautiful light, beckoning me to enter. The open door of the train emanated a bright light. Although the conductor's face was invisible, I felt an overwhelming sense of warmth, peace, and calmness. As I walked toward the open door and was about to step aboard the train, I heard the voice of the Lord above me saying, *"SEE, DIDN'T I MAKE A WAY OUT OF NO WAY?"*

Within that month, we witnessed a young man with his family evangelizing by the same train station where I had the dream. They were distributing Christian tracts. We felt an immediate connection to him. He was called to be a pastor but only had his wife and family as his congregants. Two months later, his first service was held in the basement of my parents' home, surrounded by twenty or so people. His congregation grew until we had to move into a physical building, where his ministry continued to grow and flourish.

"A WOMAN HAS NEVER WORKED HERE BEFORE"

Several years ago, during the time my sister was planning her wedding, my mother fell dangerously ill but chose to keep her condition to herself. A week after the celebrations concluded, my mother became bedridden. One afternoon, she asked if I could come by her house. Seeing her barely able to walk left me in a state of shock; it was evident that something was seriously wrong. Despite my insistence on taking her to the emergency room, she refused and instead requested that I visit the local health food store to explain her symptoms to the owner and seek his recommendations.

Upon arriving at the small health store, I anxiously looked around, hoping to find something that would alleviate my mother's discomfort. All this time, I had assumed she was suffering from gas pains, as her abdomen appeared abnormally distended for a woman of her small frame. She had also believed this to be the issue.

I meticulously explained my mother's symptoms to the clerk exactly as she had described them to me. For an entire hour and a half, we engaged in a detailed conversation as the clerk explained the various herbs and vitamins that could potentially relieve her symptoms.

Upon returning to my mother's home, I showed her the products I had purchased and shared how the store clerk—a lovely woman—had kindly provided a senior discount for her. Without hesitation, my mother got out of bed and began taking the vitamins and herbs. She felt significantly better, and I left feeling hopeful.

However, the following day, my mother called to inform me that she was experiencing severe stomach aches that had persisted throughout the night. I immediately rushed to her house, but upon my arrival, she was locked in the bathroom. When I asked how she was feeling, she assured me that she felt much better. I spent a few hours with her before leaving.

The next morning, my mother called again, this time sharing a horrifying experience. She had gone to the bathroom and, while on the commode, began vomiting. She managed to grab a bucket from under the sink and threw up congealed blood that was black in color. Simultaneously, she passed a very large black blood clot that resembled a cyst.

This continued for a while before she was able to jump in the shower and get dressed despite feeling weak. I rushed to her house, ready to call the paramedics, when she suddenly burst into praise, exclaiming, *"God has healed me."* Life seemed to have sprung back into my mother's body, and she was made perfectly whole.

After a thorough examination by her doctor, no issues were found with my mother's health. A few weeks later, she asked me to accompany her to the health food store to meet the lady who had recommended the vitamins and herbs she had taken. We waited patiently in line as the store owner attended to other customers.

When it was our turn, my mother requested to speak with the woman who had advised her daughter a few weeks earlier. The owner looked puzzled. I explained that I had spoken with a woman who recommended several items, which I then purchased, and they had significantly helped my mother.

The owner responded, *"Ma'am, I own this establishment, and I have never employed a woman here."*

I described the woman I had spoken with and mentioned that I had conversed with her for over an hour. I also noted that customers had approached the door, looked in, and then left without entering, which was unusual for such a busy store.

He reiterated, *"Ma'am, I don't know who you spoke with, but I assure you, no woman has ever worked in this store."* We left the store bewildered and confused.

My mother has shared this testimony countless times while I have pondered the experience in my heart.

This event occurred several years ago, and of all the products this remarkable lady suggested, the only one I remember is "Evening of Primrose." I always try to keep a bottle of Evening of Primrose on my shelf as a reminder of that miraculous encounter.

As Hebrews 13:2 reminds us, [2] *Be not forgetful to entertain strangers: for thereby some have entertained angels unawares.* This verse resonates deeply with our experience, suggesting that we may have encountered an angel in disguise, guiding us through a challenging time with divine wisdom and compassion.

ANGEL GUIDE

A dear friend of mine was scheduled to visit, and together with my daughter, we planned to go out for lunch. Unfortunately, she inadvertently left her phone and my home address in another pocketbook at home. Realizing this too late, she was already too far on her journey to turn back.

Despite this setback, she had a vague idea of the crossroads near my house but was unsure of the exact street number or name. After exiting the parkway, she followed a road that led her into a residential area where every intersection had a four-way stop sign.

As I waited at home, my mind was a whirlwind of worry and anticipation. I kept glancing at the clock, wondering if she would find her way or if she was lost somewhere. The minutes felt like hours, and I could not shake the feeling of unease.

Meanwhile, ahead of her vehicle, a man was driving several miles below the speed limit. She attempted to go around him, but the road was too narrow. As he approached the four-way stop sign, he slowed down even more. Then, crossing the intersection, he suddenly pulled his car to the right and parked. Exiting his vehicle, he looked back at my friend and then pointed to my house, which was diagonally across from where he was standing.

She was confused but gave him a grateful wave. He then returned to his vehicle and drove off at a normal speed. The entire encounter left her puzzled and intrigued.

Pulling into my driveway, I looked out and saw her, and

I quickly opened the door to greet her. She then asked me, *"Who was the man who directed me to your house?"* I was puzzled and asked, *"What man?"*

She then explained how she had left her phone and my address at home. She recounted how the man in the car in front of her was driving extremely slowly, but when he crossed the four-way stop sign, he pulled over, exited his vehicle, and pointed to my house.

I told her I had no idea who the man was, or how he came to know where I lived! Nevertheless, we did not hesitate to thank the Lord for His mercy toward us.

After lunch, we returned to my house and enjoyed a time of fellowship. As a prophet and an evangelist, my daughter and I held her in high regard for her respect and love for the Lord. I shared with her that my house had been on the market for over six months, and although there had been interest, the offers were consistently low.

Later that evening, as I walked her to her car, we continued our conversation. Suddenly, I saw a flame of fire emanating from the back of her heels. I quickly told her what I saw in the spirit and conveyed that the Lord was leading me to instruct her to walk around the front perimeter of my house three times while speaking in her heavenly language and laying both hands on the fence. Then, she was to walk on the pathway from the gate to the front door.

She did not question me, nor did she hesitate to follow the instructions. As she began to walk around, she laid her hands on the fence, then opened the gate and walked up the pathway to my front door. The Spirit of the Lord moved upon her mightily when her feet touched the doorstep. She shouted aloud in her voice and immediately began to break the curse that had been held against me, my family, and my house.

She revealed to me that a warlock had come to my front door, stood on the doorstep when I was unaware and placed a curse on the house so that it would not be sold.

A few months later, after signing the contract of sale, I went home for lunch one afternoon. Upon arriving, I discovered a dead black crow hidden to the side of my doorstep. The Spirit of the Lord spoke to me, instructing me to remove it using a bag and dispose of it in the garbage bucket on the curbside. Finding something suitable to pick it up with, I followed the Spirit's guidance and managed to place it into the garbage bucket just as the sanitation workers were approaching my house for pickup.

I give the Lord total thanks and praise for sending my dear sister to my house that day. An angel guided her to my home, and through her, the curse targeted against me and my family by a wicked warlock was broken. God is greater!

> 2 *As the bird by wandering, as the swallow by flying, so the curse causeless shall not come.*
>
> — PROVERBS 26:2

"WE FOOLED THEM, DIDN'T WE?"

There are two influential figures in my life whom I have always admired and felt secure around. These decent and devout men held a deep reverence for the Lord. Their presence has been profoundly significant to me, especially as they played a pivotal role in the following dream:

In my dream, I found myself in my boss's penthouse in Manhattan. Although I had never met or seen this man before, I instinctively knew in the dream that he was my boss. The penthouse featured a spacious room with a view of a charming roof deck adorned with a delightful garden.

On the opposite side of the room stood a two-door elevator, capable of transporting a person from the penthouse to the main lobby on the first floor. This setting, with its serene garden and the elevator, symbolized a journey from a place of tranquility to the bustling world below.

I exited the deck and re-entered the elegantly decorated room, proceeding to the meeting room where six of us were assembled. I took a seat in the back row, observing the others. Two rows ahead, a woman in her late forties was seated, while another woman of similar age was seated two rows in front of her. In the very front row, and slightly turned to the side, was the boss's right-hand assistant, a man about fifty years old.

To my left, at the back of the room, stood our boss, an elegant man in his late sixties, accompanied by another male assistant in his late fifties. Both men were intently focused on adjusting a projector camera in preparation for the meeting.

Suddenly, the woman seated two rows ahead of me, rose to her feet, her demeanor radiating indignation. She turned sharply to face me, her eyes ablaze with accusation. In a voice heavy with reproach, she began to reprimand me for a grievous offense I was purported to have committed—an offense of which I had no knowledge, as it was entirely fabricated.

Fear gripped me as I glanced anxiously at my boss, desperately seeking some sign of intervention or support. My heart pounded with the dread of potential dismissal, should he believe her unfounded allegations. However, he remained steadfastly focused on the camera, his gaze unwavering, his lips sealed in silence.

Amidst her vociferous accusations, I found myself repeatedly asserting, *"What are you talking about? I don't understand your allegations."* My voice, though steady, carried an undertone of desperation, seeking clarity amidst her relentless onslaughts.

In a fit of frustration, she stormed out of the room, slamming the door behind her, after realizing that the boss paid her no attention and did not engage in her banter. Fear and dread filled my heart as I was convinced that termination was imminent for me.

Unexpectedly, the woman who had been sitting two rows ahead of her, rose to her feet, her eyes piercing as she turned back to face me. With a voice filled with venom, she screamed, *"You know what she said was true, and you know exactly what she was talking about! You are the cause of the problem—you're a fraud!"* She continued to hurl accusations at me, each one more damning than the last. Still in shock, I could only respond, *"What are you talking about? I don't know what you're talking about?"*

In her frustration, she left her seat, casting a final glance at the boss. Both he and his assistant remained intently focused on the camera, their heads bowed low, without uttering a single word, as if oblivious to the accusations being hurled at me. The assistant, seated in the front row, briefly glanced at her and then at me but kept his lips sealed. She then exited the room abruptly, slamming the door behind her.

I remained seated for a moment, still consumed by the fear of being fired, before returning to the elegantly decorated room that overlooked the roof deck. I collapsed into a chair, hot tears streaming down my cheeks.

"I don't understand, Lord, what did I do wrong?" I whispered, my prayers resonating deeply within my heart. Just then, the clear tone of a bell echoed through the room, and the elevator doors suddenly slid open. To my surprise, standing to one side, ready to greet the two occupants that exited the elevator, was the boss, his face alight with elation.

The two men who emerged from the elevator bore a striking resemblance to the two influential figures I had mentioned at the beginning of the dream—figures I had always admired and felt safe around. Instinctively, I knew they were seven feet tall. Their slim build complemented their impeccable light gray suits. Their blond curly hair was almost shoulder length, and they were very good to look upon. Without a doubt, I recognized them as Angels of the Lord, identical in appearance and features, resembling twins.

The angels addressed my boss, saying, *"We fooled them, didn't we?"* I immediately understood that this conversation pertained to the two women who had falsely accused me. I also heard them say, *"It happened in the parking lot!"* followed by a shout of praise to the Lord.

One angel walked over to where I sat, leaned forward to look me in the eye, and asked, *"Why are you crying?* I fumbled for words to respond, unable to answer, before he said, *"Everything will be alright now."*

I awoke from the dream, feeling a profound sense of reassurance.

The message was undoubtedly cemented in my mind. The two women in this dream symbolized the enemy, the devil, the accuser of our faith, who relentlessly accuses us before God while whispering insidious lies in our ears:

"You're a failure; God doesn't love you; You're a fraud; God has deserted you."

The boss in the vision represents the Lord Jesus Christ, who remained unmoved and silent despite the accusations hurled at me by the devil. This steadfast focus and unwavering silence signified His divine authority and assurance, reinforcing that the enemy's accusations held no power over me.

The two assistants, as well as the two men who exited the elevator, poised and ready to follow the direction and instructions of the Lord, symbolized the angels of the Lord. They observe, guard, and protect those who are heirs of salvation, as described in Hebrews 1:14: *[14] Are they not all ministering spirits, sent forth to minister for them who shall be heirs of salvation?*

These angels never follow their own lead or move ahead of the Lord but await His directive and command.

The devil soon realized he had no control or authority over me or any of God's children. This realization led to the two women, who symbolized the devil, storming out of the room and away from His presence in total frustration. Satan, the enemy of God and our adversary, accuses believers before God, day and night, relentlessly attempting to discredit them.

> *[9] And the great dragon was cast out, that old serpent, called the Devil, and Satan, which deceiveth the whole world: he was cast out into the earth, and his angels were cast out with him.*
>
> *[10] And I heard a loud voice saying in heaven, Now is come salvation, and strength, and the kingdom of our God, and the power of his Christ: for the accuser of our brethren*

is cast down, which accused them before our God day and night.

11 And they overcame him by the blood of the Lamb, and by the word of their testimony; and they loved not their lives unto the death.

— REVELATION 12:9-11

8 Be sober, be vigilant; because your adversary the devil, as a roaring lion, walketh about, seeking whom he may devour:

9 Whom resist stedfast in the faith, knowing that the same afflictions are accomplished in your brethren that are in the world.

— 1 PETER 5:8-9

1 And he shewed me Joshua the high priest standing before the angel of the Lord, and Satan standing at his right hand to resist him.

2 And the Lord said unto Satan, The Lord rebuke thee, O Satan; even the Lord that hath chosen Jerusalem rebuke thee: is not this a brand plucked out of the fire?

— ZECHARIAH 3:1-2

In the Book of Job, Satan presents himself before God and accuses God of providing too much protection for Job, blessing him with opulence, respect, and abundance. He goes on to tell God that Job is only faithful to Him because God had blessed him with abundance, but if He were to remove that hedge of protection and remove his abundance, Job would curse God to His face:

[7] And the Lord said unto Satan, Whence comest thou? Then Satan answered the Lord, and said, From going to and fro in the earth, and from walking up and down in it.

[8] And the Lord said unto Satan, Hast thou considered my servant Job, that there is none like him in the earth, a perfect and an upright man, one that feareth God, and escheweth evil?

[9] Then Satan answered the Lord, and said, Doth Job fear God for nought?

[10] Hast not thou made a hedge about him, and about his house, and about all that he hath on every side? thou hast blessed the work of his hands, and his substance is increased in the land.

[11] But put forth thine hand now, and touch all that he hath, and he will curse thee to thy face.

— JOB 1:7-11

[1] Again there was a day when the sons of God came to present themselves before the Lord, and Satan came also among them to present himself before the Lord.

[2] And the Lord said unto Satan, From whence comest thou? And Satan answered the Lord, and said, From going to and fro in the earth, and from walking up and down in it.

[3] And the Lord said unto Satan, Hast thou considered my servant Job, that there is none like him in the earth, a perfect and an upright man, one that feareth God, and escheweth evil? and still he holdeth fast his integrity, although thou movedst me against him, to destroy him without cause.

[4] And Satan answered the Lord, and said, Skin for skin, yea, all that a man hath will he give for his life.

[5] But put forth thine hand now, and touch his bone and his flesh, and he will curse thee to thy face.

— JOB 2:1-5

[9] Yet Michael the archangel, when contending with the devil he disputed about the body of Moses, durst not bring against him a railing accusation, but said, The Lord rebuke thee.

— JUDE 1:9

The Apostle Peter refers to Satan as our "adversary" and a "roaring lion."

[8] Be sober, be vigilant; because your adversary the devil, as a roaring lion, walketh about, seeking whom he may devour.

— 1 PETER 5:8

In the Scriptures, Satan is referred to as the following:

-Prince of this world (John 12:31; 14:30; 16:11)
-The god of this world (2 Corinthians 4:4)
-Adversary (1 Peter 5:8)
-The devil (or slanderer), (Revelation 12:9);
-Murderer and liar (John 8:44)
-Angel of the bottomless pit, Abaddon or Apollyon (destroyer) (Revelation 9:11)
-Serpent (2 Corinthians 11:3)
-Dragon, old serpent, devil, Satan which deceives the whole world (Revelation 12:9)

10 Finally, my brethren, be strong in the Lord, and in the power of his might.

11 Put on the whole armour of God, that ye may be able to stand against the wiles of the devil.

12 For we wrestle not against flesh and blood, but against principalities, against powers, against the rulers of the darkness of this world, against spiritual wickedness in high places.

13 Wherefore take unto you the whole armour of God, that ye may be able to withstand in the evil day, and having done all, to stand.

14 Stand therefore, having your loins girt about with truth, and having on the breastplate of righteousness;

15 And your feet shod with the preparation of the gospel of peace;

16 Above all, taking the shield of faith, wherewith ye shall be able to quench all the fiery darts of the wicked.

17 And take the helmet of salvation, and the sword of the Spirit, which is the word of God:

18 Praying always with all prayer and supplication in the Spirit, and watching thereunto with all perseverance and supplication for all saints;

— EPHESIANS 6:10-18

Chapter 14

The Winding Down Of The Matter

As we conclude this testimony, it is my heartfelt prayer that the message of this book has touched your heart and will have a lasting, positive impact on you and those you hold dear.

One afternoon, while sitting at a traffic light, I noticed a man walking between the cars, talking to himself. He gazed up toward the heavens, pointed upward, and cried out in a loud voice, *"God help me; God help me, please! Check my records, God, please help me."* He appeared to be a retired veteran. His clothes were worn but neat—a faded military jacket over a plain shirt, and his shoes were scuffed but intact. His face was weathered, with deep lines etched by time and hardship, and his eyes, though tired, held a glimmer of hope.

As I saw him talking, I gradually opened my driver's side window to listen to what he was saying. My heart sank when I heard his prayer. The raw emotion and desperation in his voice were palpable, and I felt a profound sense of empathy for him. His plea for divine intervention was a stark reminder of the struggles many face and the enduring hope that sustains them.

I pondered deeply about his life and the challenges he might be enduring alone on the street, unaware of anyone observing or hearing his prayer. People everywhere are on a path, a journey to somewhere, yet many seem lost, unsure of their destination. They are searching for God, often in the wrong places. His appearance was not alarming, but it was evident that something weighed heavily on him as he took long, deep draws from his cigarette.

As the light turned green and I drove away, I could not shake the image of the man from my mind. His vulnerability and raw emotion were a poignant reminder of the silent struggles many endure. It made me reflect on my own journey and the times I had felt lost or in need of guidance.

In those moments of uncertainty, I found comfort in the belief that we are never truly alone. There is a higher power watching over us, ready to offer support and direction if we open our hearts and minds to it.

This encounter reinforced my conviction that we must be compassionate and attentive to those around us, for we never know the battles they are fighting.

As you finish reading this book, I hope you carry with you a renewed sense of empathy and a commitment to being a beacon of light for others. May you find strength in your faith and the courage to reach out to those in need, just as that man reached out to the heavens in his moment of need.

[5] *This then is the message which we have heard of him, and declare unto you, that God is light, and in him is no darkness at all.*

6 *If we say that we have fellowship with him, and walk
in darkness, we lie, and do not the truth:*
7 *But if we walk in the light, as he is in the light, we
have fellowship one with another, and the blood of Jesus
Christ his Son cleanseth us from all sin.*
8 *If we say that we have no sin, we deceive ourselves,
and the truth is not in us.*
9 *If we confess our sins, he is faithful and just to
forgive us our sins, and to cleanse us from all
unrighteousness.*
10 *If we say that we have not sinned, we make him a
liar, and his word is not in us.*

— 1 John 1:5-10

Notes

218 NOTES

www.ingramcontent.com/pod-product-compliance
Lightning Source LLC
LaVergne TN
LVHW050538160826
845677LV00011B/2083

* 9 7 9 8 8 9 5 6 9 3 3 2 2 *